Presented to Euan
on the occasion of his
First Communion at Balfron,
31st May, 1987.

THE GOOD NEWS
THE LIFE OF JESUS

THE GOOD NEWS

THE LIFE OF JESUS
told in the words of the evangelists
and illustrated by Franco Vasini

The Scripture texts are taken from a translation
of the New Testament by John Bligh

 St Paul Publications

Original title: *Il Vangelo - Vita di Gesù*
Compiled by Lamberto Schiatti
Layout by M. Luisa Benigni
Copyright © Edizioni Paoline, Roma 1981

St Paul Publications
Middlegreen, Slough SL3 6BT
England

English edition copyright © St Paul Publications 1981
ISBN 085439 190 8

Printed in Italy by Istituto Grafico Bertello, Borgo San Dalmazzo

St Paul Publications is an activity of the priests and brothers
of the Society of St Paul who promote the christian message
through the mass media

Britain is one of the few parts of the world where religious education is a compulsory element of the school curriculum. It is said, too, that the majority of parents want their children to have a grounding of Christian teaching. Despite this there are many in these countries (and not merely the younger members of the community) who are largely ignorant about the life of Jesus and the message of the Gospel.

I warmly recommend this carefully and attractively produced selection from the four Gospel accounts, which tells in word and picture the central part of the life and teaching of Jesus Christ. It will surely guide its readers whether Christian or non-Christian, to a clearer understanding of Christianity and a greater familiarity with the One whom Christians worship as the Son of God made Man.

DAVID KONSTANT
BISHOP IN CENTRAL LONDON

CONTENTS

Foreword   11

The gospel, the gospels and the life of Jesus   13

Prologue to the gospel   17

Incarnation and hidden life of Jesus, the Son of God   18

Public appearance of Jesus as Messiah   32

The first "week" of appearances   36

Jesus' public life   40

   The first Passover   40

   The sermon on the mount   53

   Jesus' ministry in Galilee   60

   The parables of the kingdom of God   64

   Miracles of Christ's power   68

   Mission and crisis in Galilee   74

   The second Passover   78

   The feast of Pentecost   85

   The feast of Tabernacles   92

   The feast of the Dedication of the temple 104

   The last journey to Jerusalem   106

Holy Week of the passion and death of the Lord   126

   Palm Sunday   128

   Monday in Holy Week   130

   Tuesday in Holy Week   132

   Prophetic vision of the last days   138

   Spy Wednesday   142

   Maundy Thursday: the Lord's Supper   142

   Farewell discourse   150

   Good Friday: the passion of the Lord   157

   Saturday in Holy Week   172

Resurrection of Jesus and birth of the Church   174

FOREWORD

I express myself not in words but in pictures; therefore for the foreword of this work I make room for Angela Giorgini, who has inspired me and overseen my work.

FRANCO VASINI

I have long been impressed by the feeling for people which Franco Vasini's work shows, for it allows him to treat them as fellow-beings, expressing itself in the interest he displays in the ordinary and multi-coloured crowds and in his vivid use of colour. In these crowds, brought together for a popular festival, a match, or a race-meeting, individuals are not lost but rather stand out and are recognised as people united by a common desire for festivity and life. And if in these pictures there sometimes appear traces of irony towards the people represented there, these take nothing away from their essential sincerity and joy in living; they are, as it were, the natural relief of the smile with which the poor succeed in raising the limitations of their lives.

In a human and pictorial communication of this kind, rich in brilliant colour, simple and full of confidence, there was room, it seemed to me, for the Gospel message. Therefore I suggested to Vasini that he should illustrate the Gospel, and for the same reasons the artist at once and instinctively agreed, though admitting that he had never had any close acquaintance with the text. I helped him to read some episodes and so gradually to enter into a sphere which he felt to be his own and in which he was soon stirred to independent reading and original interpretation.

The Gospel proclamation has given a new pungency to his concern for society and a new respect for its characters. The poorest person is always the most appreciative for he realises that he is undeserving of each gift and therefore becomes capable of gratitude and joy.

It can be said that the "primitive" Vasini is and knows how to make himself like his characters and, like them, is touched, amazed and delighted by the strength and sweetness of the Good News.

Everyone has blind spots which interfere with the proclamation: the apostles, who, though bathed in light, continue to sleep in the Garden of Gethsemane (as we see in that very human picture); the wise according to the flesh who went on mocking even below the cross; all sorts of people who are unmoved at the sight of Christ's passion; the foolish virgins who are amused. All these scenes are portrayed with inexhaustible imagination and painstaking vividness. Christ has chosen to live with people in every season and situation, always ready to care for them, as is shown in the nativity and a last supper realised in an idiom which is modern and full of emotion. Mary, the Mother, appears in the Pietà as the embodiment of every race and nation wounded with grief.

This work, made up of sixty canvasses, presents a unity of language and intention which bears the stamp of a mature art and a heartfelt personal interpretation of the Gospel. The theme of the light which pierces the darkness of our living returns frequently and in a moment introduces us to Another Dimension. Further, it often has *recourse to the sense of passage coupled with uncertainty which makes up the human destiny, the theme of the way. There are so many ways in the world in which the Lord has made his presence felt, through a meeting, a warning, a companionship, an encouragement, and he also appears in the picture of the mission, at the end of a path of light which comes down from heaven to bring the message of truth to the human race.*

The landscape and the skies, clearly and firmly drawn, seem to play their part in the Event, unprecedented in the world's history; the interiors, rich in colour and artifice, and the very architecture of the buildings are brought out in harmony with each message that the artist wishes to portray. Those who are familiar with the work of Vasini can testify to a sensitivity, formerly purely human, on which have been superimposed the beginnings of the light of faith, which express, in a very new and genuine language, a freer and richer encounter among human beings, and give promise of a wider Reality.

ANGELA GIORGINI

12

THE GOSPEL, THE GOSPELS AND THE LIFE OF JESUS

The word *gospel* means *good news*, and refers to the best news in all history which burst forth 2,000 years ago in Bethlehem: "*I shall bring you good tidings of great joy: today a saviour is born for you*" (Lk 2:11). Formerly, the word had been used of good news of national events, and in the Old Testament of the fulfilment of messianic prophecies: in this sense Jesus applied it to himself, in order to show that the prophecies of the kingdom of God were realised in him. In the early Church to preach the gospel meant to spread the good news that salvation and redemption in Christ were available to all; so it had a strong missionary and converting significance.

The *gospel* as we understand it today developed in three stages. First, there was the living experience of hearing the Lord unfolding his teaching according to the modes of thought and expression of his time so that it might be understood and remembered by his hearers. Next, after the resurrection, the apostles began to "bear witness" to Jesus by faithfully recalling his acts and sayings, again bearing in mind the needs and modes of expression of their various audiences. Then, to meet teaching and pastoral needs, collections of the Lord's sayings, miracles, parables, passion and death began to be made; these were finally set in order by the "evangelists" who combined the apostolic teaching with the oral instruction given in their churches. So, as St Irenaeus of Lyons records, "Matthew composed the gospel for the Hebrew people, while Peter and Paul were preaching and founding the church in Rome. After their death Mark set down in writing the essential teaching of Peter, whose disciple and secretary he had been. And Luke, a follower of Paul, composed a book of the gospel which the apostle had been preaching. Later John, the beloved disciple, also produced a gospel". The gospel-proclamation, through the inspired memory of the Church, became four-fold, the "holy four" of the prophet Ezekiel who spoke of four beings in the likenesses of a man, a lion, an ox and an eagle (whence the traditional symbols of the evangelists handed down in art).

The first three gospels are put together in a similar pattern: John the Baptist's preaching and Jesus' baptism; ministry in Galilee; journey to Jerusalem, passion, death and resurrection; the apostles' mission. They are called *synoptic* ("seen together"), and they are so similar that they seem to depend upon one another, yet there are so many omissions, additions and differences that it is clear that the evangelists did not simply copy each other: Mark completely ignores the infancy of Jesus and the sermon on the mount; Matthew does not mention the ascension; Luke alone knows the precious details of the Saviour's birth and infancy. John's gospel, written towards the end of the first century, when the synoptics were already in circulation, adds some precise details of the public life of Jesus and the exact dates and circumstances of the passion, filling in important omissions of Matthew, Mark and Luke. But the fourth gospel has always been seen as a spiritual *gospel*, a mystical testimony of a soul lost in God.

So, the four gospels have a special character as inspired recollections of eye witnesses. With them a new form of literature entered history — *popular narrative*. Before them history was aristocratic, intended for educated readers; now we have *stories* in which the characters speak in ordinary, every day language. There are two protagonists: on the one hand and pre-eminently Jesus, the Messiah, whose "myth" was written down within fifty years of his death, unlike those of the heroes of antiquity whose stories accumulated legends over hundreds of years. The gospels do not build up legends about their hero, but discretely record his story in four versions which are complementary but not contradictory. On the other hand are the people, described as real persons — poor fishermen, ordinary women, children, even the thieving tax-collector and the woman of the street — who reveal a depth of natural human feeling and failing. Like the rest of the Bible, the gospels are not concerned to be "edifying" books, all of whose characters are models of perfection, but they move the reader to wonder and personal renewal. It is impossible to read the gospels and remain unmoved.

The great use of the gospel gives scope to this original life of Jesus, illustrated with the highly coloured and lively simplicity of primitive design where Jesus triumphs among the people who surround him in the sixty pictures. They touch the soul with the converting message of the gospel and drive away the torturing fantasies of modern man.

Since the first centuries of christianity to combine the four gospels into a single story has often been tried; and today it seems particularly desirable to uncover once more the *gospel in the gospels,* so as to recover the true meaning of the many excerpts read in church and memorised, and to allow them to bear their proper fruit. So, it seemed desirable to plan this ordered reading of the gospels, stimulated by the freshness of primitive illustration. Out of many possible methods of "harmonising" the gospels we have chosen a chronological reconstruction of the life of Jesus based on the feasts mentioned by St John. We have purposely omitted explanatory commentaries and notes, confining ourselves to providing short titles of the several extracts so as not to distract the reader from contemplation of the pictures and essential meditation on the gospel text.

It has been said that the best comment on the gospel is its hundredth reading; we believe that this beautiful edition will make it more stimulating to those who read it for the first time as for the hundredth time.

14

THE GOOD NEWS
THE LIFE OF JESUS

In the beginning was the Word,
and the Word was with God, and the Word was God.
He was with God in the beginning.
All things were made through him,
and without him was made nothing that was made.
In him was life, and life was the light of men,
and the light shines in the darkness,
and the darkness did not comprehend it.

A man come, sent from God, whose name was John. He came as a
witness, to give testimony to the light, that all might believe
through him. He was not the light, but was to give testimony
to the light.

The Word was the true light which shines upon every man
who comes into the world.
He was in the world, and the world had been made through him,
yet the world did not recognise him.
He came to his own, and his own did not receive him;
but to all who did receive him and who believed in his name,
to these he gave power to become children of God,
born not of blood, nor by the will of the flesh,
nor by the will of man, but of God.
And the Word became flesh, and dwelt among us;
and we beheld his glory,
the glory that belongs to the Father's only Son,
and he was full of grace and truth.
John bore witness to him and cried:
'It is of him that I spoke when I said, "Though he comes after me,
his place is before me, because he was before me." '
Of his fullness we have all received, grace upon grace.
The Law was given through Moses,
grace and truth through Jesus Christ.
No one has yet seen God; but his only Son has made him known,
he who is in the bosom of the Father, and himself is God.

(Jn 1:1-18)

INCARNATION AND HIDDEN LIFE OF JESUS
THE SON OF GOD

In the days when Herod was king of Judea, there was a priest named Zechariah, of the Order of Abijah. His wife too was a descendant of Aaron, and her name was Elizabeth. Both were just in God's eyes, for they followed blamelessly all the commandments and ordinances of the Lord. But they had no children, for Elizabeth was barren, and both of them were advanced in years

When it was his Order's turn of duty, Zechariah was serving as priest in God's presence; lots were cast as usual, and it fell to Zechariah to go in and offer incense in the Lord's sanctuary. At the hour of the offering of incense, while great numbers of the people were praying outside, there appeared to Zechariah an angel of the Lord, standing at the right hand of the altar of incense. Zechariah was troubled by the sight and fear fell upon him. But the angel said to him: 'Have no fear, Zechariah; your prayer has been heard: your wife Elizabeth will bear you a son, and you shall name him John. He will bring joy and gladness to you, and many will rejoice over his birth; for he will be great in the sight of the Lord. He will not drink wine or strong liquor, but will be filled with the Holy Spirit, even from his mother's womb. He will turn back many of the children of Israel to the Lord their God. He will go before the Lord with the spirit and power of Elijah, to reconcile the hearts of fathers to their children, to convert the disobedient to the wisdom of just men, and to prepare for the Lord a people ready to receive him.'

Zechariah said to the angel: 'But how shall I know whether this is true? I am an old man and my wife is advanced in years.' The angel replied: 'I am Gabriel, who stands in God's presence, and am sent to speak to you and to bring these good tidings. Behold, you will be dumb and unable to speak until the day when these things come to pass, because you have not believed these words of mine, which will be proved true in their time.'

Meanwhile, the people were waiting for Zechariah, and wondering why he lingered in the sanctuary. But when he came out and could not speak to them, they understood that he had seen a vision in the sanctuary. He made signs to them, but remained without speech.

When the days of his office were over, he returned home. After this his wife Elizabeth conceived. For five months she preserved secrecy about herself, thinking, 'The Lord has done this for me: in these days he has looked upon me, and has taken away my reproach among men.'

(Lk 1:5-25)

Annunciation to Mary of the incarnation of Jesus the Son of God

In the sixth month, the angel Gabriel was sent from God to a town in Galilee called Nazareth, to a virgin betrothed to a man named Joseph, who was of the house of David. Her name was Mary. Gabriel went into her home and said to her: 'Hail, full of grace! The Lord is with you.' (Blessed are you among women!) Mary was much troubled by his words and wondered what this manner of greeting might mean. But the angel said to her: 'Have no fear Mary; you have found grace with God. Behold, you will conceive in your womb and bear a son, and you shall name him Jesus. He will be great, and will be called the Son of the Most High; and the Lord God will give him the throne of his forefather David; he will rule over the house of Jacob for ever, and his kingdom will have no end.'

Mary said to the angel: 'How will this be, since I remain a virgin?' The angel answered her: 'The Holy Spirit will come upon you, and the power of the Most High will overshadow you. And therefore the holy child to be born of you will be called God's Son. And behold, your cousin Elizabeth too has conceived a son, old as she is; she who is believed to be barren is now in her sixth month, for with God nothing will prove impossible.' Then Mary said: 'Behold the handmaid of the Lord! Be it done to me according to your word.' Then the angel left her. (Lk 1:26-38)

Mary's visit to Elizabeth. The "Magnificat"

In those days, Mary set out and went eagerly to Zechariah's home in the hill-country of Judah. She went in and greeted Elizabeth; and when Elizabeth heard her greeting, the babe leaped in her womb. Elizabeth was filled with the Holy Spirit and cried aloud: 'Blessed are you among women, and blessed is the fruit of your womb! Who am I that the mother of my Lord should come to me? Behold, when your greeting sounded in my ears, the babe in my womb leaped for joy. Blessed are you for your faith that the Lord's message will be fulfilled!' And Mary said:

'My soul gives glory to the Lord
and my spirit rejoices in God my Saviour.
He has looked on the lowliness of his handmaid,
and from this day forth all generations will call me blessed!
He who is mighty has done great things for me.
(Holy is his name!)
His mercy abides from generation to generation over those
who fear him.
He puts forth his arm in power,
and scatters men who glory in their heart's conceit.
He throws down monarchs from their thrones,
but raises up the lowly.
He loads the hungry with good things,
but sends the wealthy from him empty.

He has come to the aid of his servant Israel,
and remembered, as he promised to our fathers,
the mercy which he pledged to Abraham and to his issue for ever.'

Mary stayed with Elizabeth about three months, and then returned home. (Lk 1:39-56)

Birth of John the Baptist. The "Benedictus"

The time came for Elizabeth's delivery, and she gave birth to a son. When her neighbours and relatives heard of the great mercy which the Lord had shown her, they joined in her rejoicing; and on the eighth day, when they came for the child's circumcision, they wanted him called Zechariah, after his father. But his mother said: 'No, he is to be named John.' 'But,' they said, 'there is nobody among your kinsfolk who bears that name.' Then they asked his father, by signs, what he wished him to be called. He asked for a writing-tablet and, to the wonder of all, wrote down, 'John is his name.' At once his mouth was opened and his tongue was loosed, and he began to speak and to bless God. The neighbours were all struck with awe, and these events became the talk of the whole hill-country of Judea. All who heard of them laid them up in their hearts, wondering what was the destiny of this child. For the hand of the Lord was with him.

His father Zechariah too, was filled with the Holy Spirit and spoke in prophecy:

'Blessed by the Lord God of Israel,
for he has looked graciously upon his people and
brought them deliverance.
As he promised through the lips of his ancient prophets,
he has raised for us a beacon of salvation
in the house of his servant David,
To save us from our enemies,
and from the power of all who hate us.
To prove his fidelity to our fathers
his mindfulness of the holy covenant,
of the oaths which he swore to our father Abraham,
to deliver us from the hand of our enemies,
and to give us power to serve him without fear,
and live in holiness and justice before him
all the days of our lives.
And you, my child, will be renowned as prophet of the Most High;
you will go before the Lord to prepare his way,
To bring knowledge of salvation to the people for
the forgiveness of their sins.

Such is the loving-kindness of our God
which he will show to us,
a radiance dawning from on high, to shine on men who dwell in
death's dark shadow,
and guide our feet into the path of peace.'

The child grew up and became strong in spirit; and he lived in the desert until the day when he made his appearance before Israel.   (Lk 1:57-80)

Joseph accepts the fatherhood of Jesus acknowledging him as descendant of David

The birth of Jesus Christ came about in this way. While Mary his mother was betrothed to Joseph before they were united in marriage, she came to be with child by the Holy Spirit. Joseph who was to marry her, being a just man, and not wishing to expose her to shame, meant to put her away privately. He had come to this decision, when an angel of the Lord appeared to him in a dream, and said: 'Joseph, son of David, you need not hesitate to take Mary to be your wife; for the child conceived by her is of the Holy Spirit. She will give birth to a son, and you shall call him Jesus, for it is he who will save his people from their sins.'

All this happened in fulfilment of the word spoken by the Lord through his prophet, when he said: *Behold a virgin will conceive and bear a son, and he will be called Emmanuel* (which means 'God with us').

Joseph woke from sleep and did as the angel had commanded him; he took Mary as his wife, and he gave the name Jesus to the son whom she bore, though he had not known her.   (Mt 1:18-25)

Jesus is born in a manger in Bethlehem

In those days an edict went out from Caesar Augustus for a census to be taken of the whole world. (This census took place before Cyrinus was governor of Syria.) The people all went to be enrolled, each in his own city; and Joseph, who belonged to the house and family of David, went up from the city of Nazareth in Galilee, to be enrolled in the city of David called Bethlehem in Judea. With him went Mary his espoused wife, who was with child. While they were there, her time came, and she brought forth her first-born son; and she wrapped him in swaddling-clothes, and laid him in a manger, because there was no room for them at the inn.   (Lk 2:1-7)

22

The good news is announced to the shepherds

In the same country there were shepherds out in the open, keeping the night watches over their flocks; and behold, an angel of the Lord stood by them, and the glory of the Lord shone about them, and great fear came upon them. But the angel said to them: 'Have no fear! For behold, I bring you good tidings of great joy for all the people. A Saviour has been born for you this night, in the city of David. He is the Lord Messiah. The sign by which you will know him is this: you will find a babe wrapped in swaddling-clothes and laid in a manger.' Then suddenly there appeared with the angel a great throng of the heavenly army praising God and singing: 'Glory to God on high, and on earth peace to men in whom he is well-pleased.'

When the angels left them and went back into heaven, the shepherds said to one another: 'Come then, let us go over to Bethlehem and see this new thing which the Lord has made known to us.' They went with all haste and found Mary and Joseph, and with them the babe laid in a manger. When they had seen him, they made known what had been told them about the child; and all who heard were filled with wonder at what the shepherds told them. But Mary treasured all these memories, and pondered them in her heart. The shepherds went away giving glory and praise to God for all they had seen and heard; for they had found everything exactly as had been revealed to them.

The eighth day came, the day for his circumcision, and he was named Jesus, the name by which the angel had called him before he was conceived in the womb.

(Lk 2:8-21)

Jesus is presented in the temple and is recognised as the Messiah, Saviour of all peoples

When their days of purification had been completed as laid down in the Law of Moses, they carried Jesus up to Jerusalem to present him to the Lord, for it is decreed in the Law of the Lord that every male opening the womb shall be sacred to the Lord; they wished also to make the offering laid down in the Law of the Lord: a pair of turtle-doves or two young pigeons.

Now there was a man in Jerusalem named Simeon, a just and devout man, who lived in hope of the solace of Israel, and the Holy Spirit was upon him. He had received a revelation from the Holy Spirit that he would not see death until he had seen the Lord's Anointed. Guided by the Spirit, he came into the temple; and when the parents brought in the child Jesus, to carry out the custom of the Law for him, Simeon took him into his arms and blessed God with these words:

'Now thou dost dismiss thy servant, O Lord, in peace, for thy promise is fulfilled.
For my eyes have seen the salvation
    which thou has ordained for all the nations to behold:
A light of revelation for the Gentiles,
    and of glory for the people Israel.'

Joseph rose
and took the child
and his mother
by night, and
departed to Egypt

26

Then while his father and mother were wondering over what was being said about Jesus, Simeon blessed them and said to Mary his mother: 'Behold, this child is destined for the fall of many and for the rise of many in Israel ; he will be the object of wonder and of dispute, and through him the secret thoughts of many will be revealed. Yes, and your heart too will be pierced by a sword.'

(Lk 2:22-36)

The Messiah is recognised by the Gentiles: Magi from the East come to worship him

After the birth of Jesus, which took place at Bethlehem in Judea during the reign of Herod, Magi from the East arrived in Jerusalem, and asked: 'Where is the new-born king of the Jews? We observed his star in the East and have come to worship him.' Hearing this, King Herod was perturbed, and with him the whole of Jerusalem. He called an assembly of all the chief priests and scribes of the people, and asked them where the Messiah would be born. They replied: 'At Bethlehem in Judea; for so God says through the prophet in Scripture: *And you, Bethlehem in the land of Judea, are by no means least among the leaders of Judea; for out of you will come a leader, to shepherd my people Israel.'*

Then Herod spoke to the Magi privately and learned from them the exact date when the star had appeared. He set them on their way to Bethlehem, and said: 'Go and make exact enquiries about the child, and when you find him, bring back word to me, so that I too can go and worship him.'

After the audience with the King, they set out, and the star which they had seen in the East went ahead of them until it came to rest above the place where the child was. When they saw the star they were glad and their joy was unbounded. They entered the house, and saw the child with Mary his mother, and fell on their knees and worshipped him; and they opened their treasures and offered him gifts of gold, frankincense and myrrh. Then, as they were warned in a dream not to return to Herod, they took a different route back into their own country.

(Mt 2:1-12)

Jesus, persecuted by Herod, flees into Egypt

After they had gone, an angel of the Lord appeared to Joseph in a dream, and said: 'Rise up,' he said, 'take the child and his mother, and seek refuge in Egypt. Remain there until I tell you, because Herod intends to search for the child, to do away with him.'

Joseph therefore rose up and took the child and his mother by night and made his way into Egypt, where he remained until the death of Herod. Thus was fulfilled the word spoken by the Lord through his prophet, when he said: *From Egypt I called my son.*

(Mt 2:13-15)

28

Herod, so as to destroy Jesus, has the Bethlehem children killed

When Herod saw that he had been tricked by the Magi, enraged beyond measure, he sent his men and killed all male children of two years and under in Bethlehem itself and in all its neighbourhood, reckoning from the date he had obtained from the Magi. Then was fulfilled the word spoken through the prophet Jeremiah, when he said: *A voice was heard in Ramah, wailing and loud lamentation; the voice of Rachel bewailing her children refusing all comfort, because they are gone.* (Mt 2:16-18)

The return from Egypt. The Holy Family at Nazareth

After the death of Herod, an angel of the Lord appeared in a dream to Joseph in Egypt, and said: 'Rise up, take the child and his mother, and go into the land of Israel; for those who sought to kill the child are dead.' Joseph therefore rose up and took the child and his mother, and set out for the land of Israel. When, however, he heard that in Judea Archelaus was king in the place of his father Herod, he was afraid to go there. But he received guidance in a dream, and went away into the country of Galilee. On his arrival there, he settled in a city called Nazareth; and so fulfilled the word spoken through the prophets: *he shall be called a Nazarene.* (Mt 2:19-23)

At the age of twelve Jesus shows his mission as Son of God

His parents used to go up to Jerusalem every year for the feast of the Passover. When he was twelve years old, they went up as was usual for the festival; but when the feast days were over, and they started back, the boy Jesus stayed behind in Jerusalem. His parents did not know of it, but thought he was in the company. At the end of a day's journey they looked for him among their relatives and friends, and as they could not find him, they turned back towards Jerusalem in search of him. After three days they found him in the temple, sitting among the teachers, listening to them and asking them questions. (Everyone who heard him was amazed at the intelligence which he showed in his answers.) When the parents saw him they were greatly surprised; and his mother said to him: 'My son, why have you treated us like this? Your father and I have suffered deeply while searching for you!' He said to them: 'Why did you need to search? Surely you knew that I would be in my Father's house?' But they did not understand what his words meant. (Lk 2:41-50)

Hidden life of Jesus of Nazareth

Then he went down with them to Nazareth and was obedient to their authority. His mother treasured all these memories in her heart; and as Jesus grew older, he advanced in wisdom and in grace with God and men. (Lk 2:51-52)

I n the the fifteenth year of the reign of Tiberius Caesar, while Pontius Pilate was governor of Judea, when Herod was tetrarch of Galilee, his brother Philip tetrarch of Ituraea and Trachonitis, and Lysanias tetrarch of Abilene, when Annas and Caiaphas were High Priests, the word of God came to John son of Zechariah in the desert.

He went throughout the whole region of the Jordan, preaching a baptism of repentance for the forgiveness of sins, in fulfilment of the prophecy written in the book of Isaiah:

> *There shall be a voice crying in the desert: Prepare a way for the Lord, make a straight path for him. Every hollow must be filled up, every mountain and hill levelled down; what is crooked must be made straight, and rough ways smooth. Then all mankind shall see God's salvation.*
>
> (Lk 3:1-6)

John the Baptist proclaims that the Messiah is near

J ohn said to the crowds who were coming out to be baptized by him: 'Sons of vipers, who put it into your heads to flee before the onset of the Wrath? Produce the fruit that penance demands; do not say to yourselves, "We have Abraham for our father"; I tell you God could raise up children to Abraham out of these very stones. Even now the axe lies ready at the root of the trees; every tree that does not produce good fruit is to be cut down and thrown on to the fire.'

The crowds asked John: 'What must we do then?' He answered: 'He who has two tunics must share with him who has none, and he who has food must do the same.' Even tax-gatherers came to be baptized; they too asked him: 'Master, what must we do?' He replied: 'Extract no more than the fixed amount.' Men on military service asked him: 'And what of us, what must we do?' He answered: 'No rough handling; make no false charges; and for income be content with your pay.'

The people were full of expectation; all were privately wondering whether perhaps John himself was the Messiah. But John gave them the answer by declaring to all: 'I baptize you with water; but one who has

greater power than I is coming; I am not worthy to loosen the strap of his sandals. He will baptize you with the Holy Spirit and with fire. He has taken his winnowing-fan in his hand, to clear his threshing floor; he will gather the wheat into his barn, but will destroy the chaff in ever-burning fire.'

John gave many other exhortations and sermons to the people.

(Lk 3:7-18)

Jesus, baptized by John, is proclaimed Son of God

Then Jesus made his appearance. He came from Galilee to John at the Jordan, to be baptized by him.

John tried to dissuade him: 'It is I who need to be baptized by you,' he said, 'and do you come to me?' But Jesus replied: 'For now, let it be so; it is fitting that we should fulfil in this way all that God requires.' Whereupon John yielded.

After the baptism, as Jesus came up from the water, the heavens were opened, and he saw the Spirit of God descending like a dove and coming upon him. And a voice was heard: 'This is my beloved Son, in whom I am well pleased.'

(Mt 3:13-17)

In the wilderness, Jesus too is tempted by pleasure, wealth and power

Jesus was then led by the Spirit out into the desert, to be tempted by the devil.

He fasted forty days and nights, and at the end, when he was famished the tempter came to him and said: 'If you are God's Son, order these stones to be turned into loaves of bread.' But he answered: 'The Scripture says: *Not on bread alone shall man live, but on every word that comes from the mouth of God.*'

Then the devil took him into the holy city, and made him stand on the parapet of the temple, and said to him: 'If you are God's Son, throw yourself down; for the Scripture says: *He will give his angels charge of you, and they will bear you in their arms, lest you dash your foot against a stone.*' Jesus answered him: 'The Scripture also says: *You shall not tempt the Lord your God.*'

Again, the devil took him up on to a high mountain, and showed him all the kingdoms of the world and the glory of their kings, and he said: 'All these I will give you, if you fall down and worship me.' Then Jesus said to him: 'Away from me, Satan! The Scripture says: *You shall worship the Lord your God, and serve him alone.*'

Then the devil left him, and angels appeared and ministered to him.

(Mt 4:1-11)

This is the witness which John gave, when the Jews sent priests and levites to him from Jerusalem to ask him who he was. He confessed the truth and did not deny it; he declared: 'I am not the Messiah.' So they asked him: 'What then? Are you Elijah?' He said: 'I am not.' 'Are you the Prophet?' He answered: 'No.' So they said to him: 'Then what are you? We must have some answer for those who sent us. What account do you give of yourself?' He replied: 'I am the one whom Isaiah foretold when he spoke of *a voice crying in the desert, "Make a straight way for the Lord".*'

The Pharisees asked him (for they were Pharisees who had been sent): 'Why then do you baptize, if you are neither the Messiah, nor Elijah, nor the Prophet?' John answered: 'I baptize with water; but there is standing among you one whom you do not recognise, the one who is coming after me, the thong of whose shoe I am not fit to untie.' This took place at Bethany beyond the Jordan, where John was baptizing. (Jn 1:19-28)

John points to Jesus as the "Lamb of God", that is, a victim for sin

The next day, John saw Jesus coming towards him and said: 'Behold the Lamb of God, who will take away the sin of the world! This is he of whom I spoke when I said, "After me is coming one whose place is before me, because he was before me." I myself did not recognise him; but the reason why I came baptizing with water was that he might be revealed to Israel.' And John gave this further witness: 'I saw the Spirit coming down like a dove from heaven, and it rested on him. I myself had not recognised him; but he who sent me to baptize with water had said to me, "He upon whom you see the Spirit come down and rest —he is the one who will baptize with the Holy Spirit." I have seen, and have given my witness: This is the Son of God.' (Jn 1:29-34)

John, Andrew and Peter, already disciples of the Baptist, meet Jesus

The next day, John was again standing there, and two of his disciples were with him, when Jesus passed by. John looked at him and said: 'Behold the Lamb of God!' The disciples heard him say this, and they followed Jesus.

Jesus turned round, saw them following, and said to them: 'What are you looking for?' 'Rabbi,' they said, 'where are you staying?' ("Rabbi" means "Master".) 'Come,' he replied, 'and you will see.' So they went and saw where he was staying, and they stayed with him for the rest of the day. This was at about four in the afternoon. Andrew, Simon Peter's brother, was one of the two who had heard John's word and followed Jesus. He sought out first his own brother Simon, and said to him: 'We have found the Messiah!' ("Messiah" means "the Anointed") and he brought him to Jesus. Jesus looked at him and said: 'You are Simon, son of John; your name will be Cephas.' ("Cephas" means "Rock".)

(Jn 1:35-42)

Jesus meets Philip and Nathanael in Galilee

The next day, Jesus decided to leave for Galilee. He sought out Philip and said to him: 'Follow me!' (Philip too was from Bethsaida, the home of Andrew and Peter.) Philip sought out Nathanael and said to him: 'We have found the man foretold by Moses in the Law and by the prophets: Jesus son of Joseph, from Nazareth.' Nathanael replied: 'From Nazareth? Can anything good come from there?' Philip said to him: 'Come and see!' Jesus saw Nathanael coming to him and said of him: 'Here is a true Israelite, in whom there is no guile!' Nathanael exclaimed: 'How did you come to know me?' Jesus answered: 'I saw you under the fig tree, before Philip called you.' Nathanael exclaimed: 'Rabbi, you are the Son of God! You are the king of Israel!' Jesus answered: 'Because I said to you, "I saw you under the fig tree," you believe; but you will see greater things than that.' And he added: 'I tell you truly, you will behold heaven opened wide and the angels of God ascending and descending over the Son of Man.'

(Jn 1:43-51)

Jesus begins his ministry with his first miracle at Cana in Galilee

On the third day, a marriage was being celebrated at Cana in Galilee, at which the mother of Jesus was present. Jesus himself and his disciples were among the wedding-guests. As the wine had run short, Jesus' mother said to him: 'They have no wine.' But Jesus said to her: 'Woman, what is it to you and me? My hour is not yet come.' His mother said to the servants: 'Do whatever he tells you.' There were standing there (for the Jewish rites of purification) six stone water-jars, each of which would hold about twenty gallons. Jesus said to the servants: 'Fill up those jars with water.' And they filled them to the brim. Then he said to them: 'Now draw some off, and take it to the chief servant,' and they did so. When the chief servant had tasted the water which had turned into wine, since he did not know where it came from (only the servants who had drawn the water knew), he called out to the bridegroom: 'It is usual to offer the better wine first, and the less good when people are drunk; but you have kept the better wine till now.' In this miracle, which he did at Cana in Galilee, the first of his signs, Jesus revealed his glory; and his disciples believed in him.

After this, Jesus went down to Capernaum with his mother and his brethren and his disciples, and stayed there a few days.   (Jn 2:1-12)

When the Jewish Passover was near, Jesus went up to Jerusalem. In the very temple he found traders selling cattle and sheep and doves, and money-changers sitting at their tables. So he made a whip of ropes and drove them all out of the temple with their sheep and cattle; he scattered the coins of the money-changers and overturned their tables; and he said to the sellers of doves: 'Away with these things! Out of here! Would you turn my Father's house into a bazaar?' And the disciples remembered that the Scripture says: *Zeal for your house will consume me.* Then the Jews retorted: 'What right have you to do this? Show us some sign!' Jesus answered: 'Destroy this temple, and in three days I will raise it up. The Jews said: 'This temple has taken forty-six years to build, and will you raise it up in three days?' But Jesus was speaking of the temple of his body. After he had risen from the dead, his disciples remembered that he had said this, and they put their faith in the Scripture and in the word that Jesus had spoken.

THE FIRST PASSOVER

During Jesus' stay in Jerusalem for the Passover and the feast days, many people put their faith in his name because they saw the signs that he was performing. Jesus, however, put no faith in them, because he knew what all men are; he had no need for anyone to tell him what man is; he knew what is in man.

(Jn 2:13-25)

Conversation with Nicodemus: to be Christian means to be born again, to change one's life

A Pharisee, called Nicodemus, who was one of the Jewish rulers, came to Jesus at night and said: 'Rabbi, we know that you are a teacher who has come from God — because no one can do signs such as you are doing unless God is with him.' Jesus replied: 'I will tell you truly, unless a man is reborn from above, he cannot see the kingdom of God.' Nicodemus said: 'But how is it possible for a man to be born when he is old? Surely he cannot go back into his mother's womb and be born a second time?' Jesus answered: 'I tell you truly, unless a man is born of water and Spirit, he cannot enter the kingdom of God. What is born of the flesh is flesh, and what is born of the Spirit is spirit. You ought not to be astonished when I say that you must be reborn from above. The Spirit is like the wind, which blows where it wills; you hear

the sound of it, but you do not know where it is coming from or where it is going. So it is with everyone who is born of the Spirit.'

Nicodemus asked: 'But how can this come about?' Jesus replied: 'Are you a master of Israel and yet unaware of this? I tell you truly, we speak of what we know, and we bear witness to what we have seen; and yet you do not accept our witness. I have told you things on earth and you do not believe them; how then will you believe if I tell you of heavenly things?

'No one has been up in heaven — only he who came down from heaven, the Son of Man. As Moses raised up the serpent in the desert, so must the Son of Man be raised up, in order that everyone who believes in him may have eternal life. For God so loved the world that he gave up his only-begotten Son, in order that everyone who believes in him may not perish but have eternal life. For God sent his Son into the world, not to condemn the world, but that the world might be saved through him. He who believes in him escapes condemnation; he who does not believe is condemned already, because he has not believed in the name of the only Son of God. This is the Judgement: the Light has come into the world and men have preferred darkness to the Light, because of their evil works. Whoever does evil shuns the light and refuses to come into it, for he fears to have his works shown up; but the man who lives by truth comes into the light, so that it may be clearly seen that his works have been done in God.'

(Jn 3:1-21)

Last public witness of John the Baptist

After this, Jesus went into Judea, and stayed there with his disciples, and began to baptize. John too was baptizing at Aenon near Salim, because water was plentiful there, and people kept coming to be baptized. For at this time John had not yet been thrown into prison. A dispute arose between John's disciples and a Jew about purification. So they went to John and said to him: 'Rabbi, the man who was with you across the Jordan, the one to whom you bore witness, is now baptizing and everyone is going to him.' John replied: 'A man can receive only what is given him from heaven. You yourselves can testify that I said, "I am not the Messiah, but only his forerunner." It is the bridegroom who has the bride; the bridegroom's friend, who stands and listens, finds his joy in hearing the bridegroom's voice. Such is the joy which I now have in full measure. He must wax and I must wane.'

(Jn 3:22-30)

Talk with the
Samaritan woman:
Jesus the Messiah
promises the water
of life

A report had now reached the ears of the Pharisees that Jesus was converting and baptizing more disciples than John (although it was not Jesus himself who did the baptizing, but his disciples). When Jesus heard of this, he left Judea and went back into Galilee. His journey took him through Samaria, and he came to a Samaritan town called Sychar, close to the piece of land which Jacob gave to his son Joseph. On it is Jacob's Well. Jesus, who was tired after the journey, sat down beside this well. It was about mid-day. A Samaritan woman came to draw water, and Jesus said to her: 'Give me a drink.' (For his disciples had gone into the town, to buy provisions.) The Samaritan woman said: 'What makes a Jew like you ask me for a drink? I am a Samaritan!' (For Jews do not use the same vessels as Samaritans.)

Jesus said to her: 'If you knew the gift that God offers, and who it is that is asking you for a drink, it is you who would have asked him. And he would have given you a living water.' The woman answered: 'Sir, you have no means of drawing water, and the well is deep; If then you have living water, where does it come from? Or are you someone greater than our father Jacob, who gave us the well, and drank from it himself, and his sons too, and his cattle?' Jesus replied: 'Everyone who drinks this water will be thirsty again; but once a man drinks the water that I shall give him, he will never thirst again. The water I shall give him will become an ever-flowing fountain of life-giving water within him.' The woman said to him: 'Sir, give me this water, then I shall never be thirsty, and shall not have to keep coming here to draw water.'

Jesus replied: 'Go and fetch your husband, and then come back.' The woman replied: 'I have no husband.' Jesus said to her: 'You are right to say, "I have no husband." You have had five, and the man you have now is not your husband; you have spoken the truth.' The woman said to him: 'Sir, I see that you are a prophet. Tell me, then, our forefathers worshipped on this mountain, yet you Jews say that the temple in Jerusalem is the place for worship.' Jesus replied: 'Believe me, woman, the hour is coming when you will worship the Father neither on this mountain nor in Jerusalem. You worship what you do not know; we worship what we do know; that is why salvation is to go forth from the Jews. But the hour is coming, and indeed is now here, when true worshippers will worship the Father in Spirit and truth; such are the worshippers whom the Father wants. God is Spirit, and his worshippers must worship him in Spirit and truth.' The woman said to him: 'I know that the Messiah is to come (that is, the Christ); when he comes, he will tell us all that is to be done.' Jesus said: 'I am he, I who am talking to you!' (Jn 4:1-26)

Jesus, the obedient
Messiah, acknowledged
as Saviour of
the world

At this moment, his disciples came back. They were surprised that he was conversing with a woman, but no one asked him what he wanted or why he was conversing with her. Then the woman left her water-jar, and went into the town and said to the people: 'Come and see a man who has told me all that I have done. Perhaps he is the Messiah!' So they left the town, to come and see Jesus.

Meanwhile, his disciples began pressing him to eat: 'Rabbi,' they said, 'take some food.' But he answered: 'Though you do not know it, I have food to eat.' So the disciples began to say to one another: 'Perhaps someone has brought him food.' Jesus said to them: 'Doing the will of him who sent me is my food, and bringing his work to completion. You say (do you not?), "Still four months before the harvest comes." I tell you, lift up your eyes and look: the fields are ripe for the harvest already. He who reaps the harvest receives his wages and gathers in a crop for eternal life; and thus both sower and reaper will rejoice together. For here the proverb holds good that "One sows and another reaps." I sent you to reap a harvest for which you have not laboured. Others have laboured, and you have come in to reap the harvest of their work.'

Many of the inhabitants of that Samaritan town had believed in Jesus because of the woman's word when she assured them that he had told her all she had done. So when they came to him they asked him to make a stay with them. He stayed there two days, and many more believed in him because of his own word; and they said to the woman: 'Our belief no longer rests on your report; we have heard him ourselves, and we know the truth: this is the Saviour of the world.'

After the two days Jesus left, and went up into Galilee. For he himself had testified that a prophet is not honoured in his own country. When he arrived in Galilee, the Galileans welcomed him, because they had seen all that he did at Jerusalem during the feast. For they too had been there for the feast.

(Jn 4:27-45)

Jesus begins his
public preaching
and calls his
first disciples
in Galilee

When Jesus heard that John had been imprisoned, he retired into Galilee. He left Nazareth, and went and settled in Capernaum by the Sea, in the territory of Zebulun and Naphtali. Thus was fulfilled the word spoken through the prophet Isaiah, when he said:

Land of Zebulun, land of Naphtali,
way of the Sea, country beyond the Jordan,
Galilee of the Gentiles!
The people that dwelt in darkness
have seen a great light;
on those who lived in the region of death's shadow
its rays have dawned.

It was from this time that Jesus began his preaching: 'Repent!' he said, 'for the kingdom of heaven is near!'

While walking beside the Sea of Galilee, he saw two brothers, Simon who is called Peter, and his brother Andrew, both fishermen, casting a net into the sea; he said to them: 'Come, follow me, and I will make you fishers of men,' and at once they left their nets and followed him. Then he went on and saw another pair of brothers, James son of Zebedee, and his brother John, in a boat with their father Zebedee, putting their nets in order. He called them, and at once they left the boat and their father, and followed him.

Then Jesus went round the whole of Galilee, teaching in the synagogues, proclaiming the good news of the kingdom, and curing every disease and every illness among the people. His fame spread throughout Syria, and all who were ill, sufferers from every kind of sickness and pain, demoniacs, lunatics and paralytics, all were brought to him, and he cured them. Great crowds accompanied him from Galilee, the Decapolis, Jerusalem, Judea and Transjordania.

(Mt 4: 12-25)

Jesus, at Cana in
Galilee, rewards the
faith of a royal
official

So he came back to Cana in Galilee, where he had turned the water into wine. Now there was a royal officer whose son was lying ill at Capernaum. When he heard that Jesus had come up from Judea into Galilee, he came to him and begged him to go down and cure his son, who was at the point of death. Jesus said to him: 'Unless you people see signs and wonders, you refuse to believe.' The officer said to him: 'Lord, come down before my boy dies.' Jesus replied: 'Go home; your son shall live.' The man believed the word that Jesus had spoken, and went home.

While he was still on his way back, his servants came to meet him with the news that his child was better. He asked them what time it was when he had recovered, and they replied: 'Yesterday, at one in the afternoon, the fever left him.' Then the boy's father knew that he had recovered at the very time when Jesus had said to him, 'Your son shall live.' So he and all his household became believers. This, then, was the second sign which Jesus performed, after he had come from Judea into Galilee.

(Jn 4:46-54)

Jesus teaches with authority, and cures a man possessed by a demon

They went into Capernaum; and on the sabbath he entered the synagogue and taught there. The people were amazed at his teaching, because he was teaching them as one with power, and not like the scribes.

A man possessed by an unclean spirit was present in the synagogue. He cried out: 'What have you to do with us, Jesus of Nazareth? Have you come to destroy us? I know who you are — the Holy One of God!' Jesus rebuked him: 'Be silent!' he said, ' and go out of him!' Then the unclean spirit threw the man into convulsions, gave a loud cry, and went out of him. Everyone was astonished; they asked one another: 'What is this? A new teaching invested with power! Why, even unclean spirits obey his word of command!' And the report of him quickly spread everywhere throughout the district of Galilee.

(Mk 1:21-28)

Jesus cures Peter's mother-in-law, and many resort to him

After the meeting in the synagogue, Jesus came out and went to the house of Simon and Andrew, with James and John. Simon's mother-in-law was lying ill with a fever; so they told Jesus about her. He went to her, took her by the hand and raised her up; the fever left her, and she began to wait on them.

In the evening, when the sun had set, they brought to him all who were sick or possessed; and the whole town was gathered round the door. He cured many who were suffering from various diseases, and cast out many devils; but he did not allow the devils to speak, because they knew who he was.

In the morning, he rose long before day-break, and went out to a lonely place, and there gave himself to prayer. Simon and his companions went in search of him, and when they found him, they said to him: 'Everyone is looking for you.' But he answered: 'Let us go on to the next towns and villages, so that I can preach there too; that is what I have come to do.' Then he travelled throughout Galilee, preaching in the synagogues and casting out devils.

(Mk 1:29-39)

Jesus preaches from Peter's boat, and calls the first disciples to remain with him

Once when Jesus was standing by the side of Lake Gennesaret and the crowd was pressing about him to hear the word of God, he saw two small boats riding at the water's edge; the fishermen had come ashore and were washing their nets. One of the boats was Simon's; Jesus boarded it and asked Simon to put off a little from the shore. Then he sat down and taught the people from the boat.

When he had finished speaking, he said to Simon: 'Head out into the deep water, and lower your nets for a catch.' Simon answered: 'Master, we worked all night long and caught nothing, but since you give the word, I will lower the nets.' They did so, and took a huge haul of fish. Their nets were almost breaking, so they made signals to their partners in the other boat to come and help them. They came and filled both boats to the point of sinking. When Simon Peter saw this, he fell at Jesus' knees and said: 'Go away from me, Lord; I am a sinner.' He and all his crew were seized with awe over the catch of fish they had made; so too were James and John, the sons of Zebedee, who were Simon's partners. But Jesus said to Simon: 'Have no fear; from now on you will catch men.' They beached the boats, then left everything and followed Jesus.

(Lk 5:1-11)

Jesus cleanses a leper so that he may return to life with others

A leper came to Jesus and knelt down and begged his aid: 'If it is your will,' he said, 'you can make me clean.' Jesus' heart was moved with pity; he stretched out his hand and touched him: 'It is my will;' he said, 'be made clean!' At once the leprosy left the man, and he was made clean. Jesus spoke sternly and sent him away: 'See that you say nothing to anyone,' he said, 'but go and show yourself to the priest, and make an offering for your purification as Moses laid down, for the priests' information.' But the man went away and freely proclaimed his cure, and spread the story everywhere, with the result that Jesus could no longer enter a town openly, but had to remain outside in deserted places. Yet people continued to come to him from all sides. (Mk 1:40-45)

The paralytic at Capernaum: Jesus heals soul and body since he can forgive sins

Some days later, he returned to Capernaum. The news spread that he was at home, and the crowd which gathered was so great that there was no room left even outside the door. While he was preaching the Word to them, some men came with a paralytic, carried by four bearers. As they were unable to bring him close to Jesus because of the throng, they removed the roofing above where he was, and cleared an opening and let down the stretcher with the paralytic lying on it. Jesus saw their faith and said to the paralytic: 'My son, your sins are forgiven.' Some scribes who were sitting there began thinking in their hearts: 'Why does he speak like this? He is blaspheming! Who but God alone can forgive sins?' But Jesus knew in his spirit that they were privately thinking these thoughts, so he said to them: 'Why do you allow these thoughts to enter your hearts? Which is easier: to say to the paralytic, "Your sins are forgiven," or to say, "Rise, take up your stretcher, and walk!"? However, to show you that the Son of Man has power to forgive sins on earth (here he turned to the paralytic), I bid you, rise up, take your stretcher and go home.' He stood up, and took his stretcher, and went out with everyone watching. All were astonished and gave glory to God: 'Never,' they said, 'have we seen anything like it!' (Mk 2:1-12)

Jesus calls Matthew (or Levi) to follow him, and eats with sinners

Again he went out by the seaside, and all the people kept coming to him, and he continued to teach them.

As he passed on, he saw Levi son of Alphaeus, sitting in the customs house. He said to him: 'Follow me!' and Levi rose and followed him.

Jesus was taking a meal in his house, and many tax-gatherers and sinners sat down with him and his disciples (there were many of these and they used to accompany Jesus from place to place). Some scribes who were also Pharisees saw that he was eating with sinners and tax-gatherers, and said to his disciples: 'What does he mean by eating with tax-gatherers and sinners?' Jesus heard this and said to them: 'It is not healthy men who need a doctor, but those who are ill. I have come to call not just men, but sinners.' (Mk 2:13-17)

Being with Jesus is joyful: keeping precepts is like useless tinkering

The disciples of John and the Pharisees were fasting. So people came to Jesus and said: 'How is it that the disciples of John fast, and the disciples of the Pharisees, but not yours?' Jesus answered: 'Surely the bridegroom's friends cannot fast while the bridegroom is still with them? No! They cannot be expected to fast so long as they have the bridegroom with them. However, the time will come when the bridegroom will have been taken away from them, and then they will fast, when that day comes!'

'You do not sew a patch of new cloth onto an old coat, or else the new piece pulls away from the old and a worse tear is made. And you do not pour new wine into old wine-skins: or else the wine will burst the skins, and both wine and skins are lost. New wine must be poured into fresh skins!'

(Mk 2:18-22)

God's law is made for men and women; not the reverse

Jesus was once going through cornfields on the sabbath, and his disciples were plucking ears of corn as they walked along. At this the Pharisees said to him: 'Look! Why are they doing what is not lawful on the sabbath?' He answered: 'Have you never read what David did when he and his men were in need and hungry — how he went into God's house, in the time of the High Priest Abiathar, and ate the shew-bread, which the Law does not allow anyone except the priests to eat, and how he also gave some of it to his men?' And he added: 'The sabbath was made for man, not man for the sabbath. Therefore the Son of Man has authority even over the sabbath!'

(Mk 2:23-28)

The man with the withered hand: good works do not break the sabbath rest

Another time he went into a synagogue, and among those present was a man with a withered hand. They were watching to see if he would cure him on the sabbath, for they wanted a charge to bring against him. He said to the man with the withered hand: 'Rise up, and come out in the middle!' Then he asked them: 'Which is it lawful to do on the sabbath, good or evil — to save a life or to put to death?' But they remained silent. Jesus looked round at them with anger, and grieved over the hardness of their hearts. He then said to the man: 'Stretch out your hand!' He did so, and his hand was restored. At once the Pharisees went out and joined with Herod's courtiers in plotting against him, to make an end of him.

(Mk 3:1-6)

Jesus chooses twelve apostles

About this time, he went out on to the mountain to pray, and spent the night there in prayer to God. When day came he [. . .] called those whom he wanted, and they went to him. He appointed twelve to be his companions, to be sent out to preach, and to have power to cast out devils. The Twelve he appointed were: Simon (to whom he gave the name Peter), then James son of Zebedee, and John the brother of James (to these he gave the name Boanerges, that is, sons of thunder), then Andrew, and Philip, and Bartholomew, and Matthew, and Thomas, and James the son of Alphaeus, and Thaddaeus, and Simon the Zealot, and Judas Iscariot, who later betrayed him.

(Lk 6:12-13; Mk 3:13-19)

THE SERMON ON THE MOUNT

The new law for the new people of God

When Jesus saw the crowds, he went up the mountain. He sat down, and when his disciples had gathered about him, he gave them this teaching.

Blessed are the poor in spirit, for theirs is the kingdom of heaven.
Blessed are those who mourn, for they shall be comforted.
Blessed are the meek, for they shall inherit the earth.
Blessed are those who hunger and thirst for justice, for they shall be satisfied.
Blessed are the merciful, for they shall be treated with mercy.
Blessed are the pure of heart, for they shall see God.
Blessed are the makers of peace, for they shall be called God's sons.
Blessed are those who suffer persecution for the sake of justice, for theirs is the kingdom of heaven.

'Count yourself blessed when they insult you, and persecute you, and calumniate you in every way because of me. Be glad of it and rejoice, for you will have a great reward in heaven. They persecuted the prophets before you in just this way.'
(Mt 5:1-12)

Christianity must shine out to give meaning to life

'You are the salt of the earth. (But if salt loses its taste, what will you use to restore its saltiness? It is no longer good for anything except to be thrown out and trodden under men's feet.) You are the light of the world. A city built on a mountain-top cannot but be seen.

'When a lamp is lit, it is not put under a barrel, but on a lampstand; then its gives light to everyone in the house. You too, in the same way, must let your light shine out before men, so that they will see your good works and give glory to your Father in heaven.'
(Mt 5:13-16)

The new law surpasses and completes the old one

'Do not imagine that I have come to abolish the Law or the prophets; I have come not to abolish, but to fulfil. (For I tell you truly, until heaven and earth pass away, not one jot or tittle of the Law will pass away — until all is fulfilled.) Whoever, therefore, relaxes one of the least of these commandments, and teaches others to do so, will be accounted least in the kingdom of heaven; but whoever keeps them and teaches others to keep them will be accounted great in the kingdom of heaven. For I tell you that unless you far surpass the scribes and Pharisees in justice, you will not enter the kingdom of heaven at all.'
(Mt 5:17-20)

It is not enough to refrain from killing: hating is like killing

'You have taken literally the commandment given to the men of old, *You shall not kill*, as meaning that whoever commits murder shall be liable to judgement. But I tell you that anyone who is angry with his brother will be liable to judgement; whoever scorns his brother will be brought before the court; and whoever calls him a godless fool will suffer the fires of hell.

'If you are at the altar, making an offering, and while there you remember that your brother has a grievance against you, leave your offering in front of the altar. Go off and make peace with your brother first, then return and make your offering.

'Settle quickly with your adversary while on your way to court, or perhaps he will hand you over to the judge, and the judge to the police, and you will be thrown into prison. I tell you truly, you will not be released until you have paid every penny.' (Mt 5:21-26)

Real loyalty, like real disloyalty, is from the heart

'You have taken literally the commandment: *You shall not commit adultery*. I tell you that anyone who looks at a woman with desire has already committed adultery with her, in his heart.
'If your right eye causes you to sin, pluck it out, throw it away! Better for you that one part of your body should perish, than that the whole of it be thrown into hell. If your right hand causes you to sin, chop it off, throw it away! Better for you that one part of your body should perish than that the whole of it go into hell.' (Mt 5:27-30)

Divorce is adultery if the marriage is valid and legal

'It was laid down that *whoever puts away his wife must give her a certificate of divorce*. But I tell you that to put away your wife, unless your "marriage" was adultery, is to make an adultress of her, and to marry a woman who is separated from her husband is to commit adultery.' (Mt 5:31-32)

Simple truth is better than much swearing

'You have taken literally the commandments given to the men of old: *You shall not swear false oaths*, and *You must keep the oath that you have sworn to the Lord*. I tell you not to swear oaths at all — not by heaven, for it is the throne of God; nor by earth, for it is his footstool; nor by Jerusalem, for it is the Great King's city. And do not swear by your own head, because you cannot turn a single hair white or black. But let your word be plain Yes when you mean Yes, and No when you mean No; anything beyond this is from the evil one.' (Mt 5:33-37)

Tolerance is better then vengeance or rigid justice

'You have taken literally the rule, *an eye for an eye and a tooth for a tooth*. But I now tell you not to resist one who is evil. If struck on the right cheek, turn the other cheek. If a man wants to go to law and take your tunic from you, give him your cloak as well. If anyone presses you to accompany him one mile, go two. Give when asked, and do not turn away from one who wants to borrow.' (Mt 5:38-42)

The Christian revolution includes love even of one's enemies

'You have taken the commandment, *You shall love your neighbour* as meaning 'You may hate your enemy'. I say to you: love your enemies and pray for those who persecute you; then you will be true sons of your Father in heaven; for he makes his sun rise upon bad men and good, and sends rain upon just men and unjust. If you love only those who love you, what reward is due to you? Do not even the tax-gatherers do that? Do not even Gentiles do that? You must, therefore, be perfect in the same way as your heavenly Father is perfect.'

(Mt 5:43-48)

Doing good does not need to be talked about

'Be careful not to perform your religious duties publicly to win the admiration of men; otherwise you have no reward laid up with your Father in heaven.

'Thus, when you give alms, do not have a trumpet blown before you, as the hypocrites do in the synagogues and streets, in order to win praise from men. I tell you truly, they have their reward already. You, when you give alms, must not let your left hand know what your right is doing; if your almsgiving is done secretly, your Father who sees what is secret will repay you.' (Mt 6:1-4)

The "Our Father" is the prayer of Christians

'When you pray, you must not be like the hypocrites, who love to stand at prayer in the synagogues and at street corners, where they can be seen and admired by men. I tell you truly, they have had their reward already. You, when you pray, must go into your inner room and shut the door and pray to your Father who is in secret, and your Father who sees what is secret will repay you.'

'When you pray, do not gabble like Gentiles. They think they will gain a hearing by heaping up words. Do not be like them. For your heavenly Father knows what you need before you ask him. This is the way for you to pray:

> Our Father, who art in heaven,
> hallowed be thy name;
> thy kingdom come,
> thy will be done,
> on earth as it is in heaven.
> Give us this day our daily bread.
> And forgive us our trespasses,
> as we forgive those who trespass against us.
> And lead us not into temptation,
> but deliver us from evil.

'For if you forgive other men their trespasses, your heavenly Father will forgive you yours; but if you do not forgive other men, your Father will not forgive you your trespasses either.' (Mt 6:5-15)

Ostentation ruins sacrifice: real treasure is in heaven

'When you fast, do not put on a mournful face, as the hypocrites do; they put on a gaunt look, to let other men see that they are fasting. As for reward, I tell you, they have had it already. You, when you fast, must oil your hair and wash your face, so that other men will not notice that you are fasting, but only your Father who is in secret; and your Father who sees what is secret will repay you.

'Do not collect precious things for yourself on earth, where moth and rust will spoil, or thieves break in and steal them; pile up your treasure in heaven, where there is neither moth nor rust to spoil, nor thieves to break in and steal. For where your treasure is, there your heart will be too.' (Mt 6:16-21)

Inner clearness illuminates life. Either God or riches

'The lamp of the body is the eye. If your eye is generous, your whole body will be lit up; but if your eye is grudging, your whole body will be filled with darkness. If then the very light within you is darkness, how deep will the darkness be!

'No man can be the faithful servant of two masters. He will end up with loathing for one and love for the other, or (if you prefer) with loyalty for one and contempt for the other. You cannot serve God and also serve Money.' (Mt 6:22-24)

For anyone who believes in God what is right must be the first priority

'That is why I say to you, do not be anxious about what you eat or drink for the support of your life, nor about what clothes you wear for the good of your body: is not your life something greater than its food, and your body something greater than its clothing? Look at the birds of the air: they do not sow or reap or gather into barns, yet your heavenly Father looks after them. Are you not much more valuable than they are? And which of you, by putting his mind to it, could add eighteen inches to his height? Why are you anxious about your clothes? Look at the lilies of the field and how they grow: they do not labour, they do not spin; and yet I tell you, not even Solomon in all his glory was dressed as splendidly as one of these! If then God clothes in this way the grass of the field, which lives today and tomorrow is thrown into the oven, will he not do even more for you, men of little faith? Then do not ask, "What are we going to eat?" or "What are we going to drink?" or "What are we going to wear?" Those are the things the Gentiles are bent upon. Do not give way to anxiety, for your heavenly Father is aware that you need all these things. Seek first the kingdom (of God) and his justice; then all these things will be given to you in addition. Do not be anxious about tomorrow; let tomorrow take care of its own troubles. Today has always enough of its own.'   (Mt 6:24-34)

Do not judge, so that God may not judge you

'Refrain from judging others, and you will not be judged. For as you judge, so you will be judged; the measure you use for others will be used for you in return.

'How is it that you see the speck in your brother's eye, yet fail to notice the beam in your own? Or how can you say to your brother, "Allow me to remove the speck from your eye," when all the time there is a beam in your own? Hypocrite! First remove the beam from your own eye, and then you will see well enough to remove the speck from your brother's.'
(Mt 7:1-5)

The virtue of discretion: prayer is the strength of Christians

'Do not give what is holy to dogs; and do not cast your pearls before swine, or they will trample them underfoot, and turn and savage you.

'Ask, and your request will be granted; seek, and you will find; knock, and the door will be opened to you. It is always he who asks that receives, and he who seeks that finds; and to him who knocks the door will be opened. Is there a man among you who will hand his son a stone when he asks him for bread or a snake when he asks for fish? If then you, bad as you are, know how to give good things to your children, how much more will your Father in heaven give good things to those who ask him.

'Always behave towards others as you would have them behave towards you. This rule sums up the Law and the Prophets.' (Mt 7:6-12)

58

Life lived comfortable and with little effort brings death: just saying prayers is not enough

'Enter by the narrow gate. For the gate that leads to destruction is wide, the road is broad, and many go that way; but the gate that leads to life is narrow, the road is difficult, and those who find it are few.

'Beware of false prophets! They come to you clad in sheep's clothing, but beneath it are ravening wolves.

'By their fruits you will know them. Does one gather grapes off thorn bushes or figs off thistles? No! But good fruit always means a good tree, and bad fruit a rotten one. Bad fruit cannot come from a good tree, nor good fruit from a rotten tree. When a tree does not yield sound fruit, it is cut down and thrown on the fire. So then by their fruits you will know them.

'It is not those who say to me "Lord, Lord," who will go into the kingdom of heaven, but those who do the will of my Father in heaven. Many will say to me on that day, "Lord, Lord, did we not prophesy in your name, and expel devils in your name, and work many miracles in your name?" But I shall say to them, "I have never known you; depart from me, you whose works were evil".'   (Mt 7:13-23)

To hear God's word is not enough: it must be put into practice

'Everyone therefore who hears these words of mine and obeys them will be like a wise man who built his house on rock:
the rain fell,
and torrents came,
and winds blew
and beat against that house,
but it did not collapse,
because its foundations were on rock.

But anyone who hears these words of mine and does not obey them will be like a foolish man who built his house upon sand:

the rain fell, and torrents came,
and winds blew
and battered that house,
and it collapsed,
and its downfall was complete.'

When Jesus finished speaking these words, the crowds were amazed at his teaching; for he taught them as one invested with authority, and not like their scribes.   (Mt 7:24-29)

59

JESUS' MINISTRY IN GALILEE

The centurion of Capernaum

When he went into Capernaum, a centurion came to him with this entreaty: 'Lord, my boy is stricken down at home with paralysis, and is in great pain.' Jesus said to him: 'I will come and cure him.' But the centurion answered: 'Lord, I am not worthy to receive you under my roof. I know you have only to say the word, and my boy will be cured. I myself am a man subject to authority, and I have soldiers under me: I say to this one "Go," and he goes, and to another "Come," and he comes, and to my slave, "Do this," and he does it.' When Jesus heard this, he was amazed and said to his followers: ' I tell you truly, I have not found such great faith in Israel! I tell you many will come from east and west, and take their places with Abraham and Isaac and Jacob in the kingdom of heaven; but the heirs of the kingdom will be banished to the darkness outside, where there will be weeping and gnashing of teeth! Then Jesus said to the centurion: 'Go; as you have believed, so be it done for you.' And the boy was cured at that very hour.

(Mt 8:5-13)

Jesus raises to life the widow's son at Nain

Soon afterwards Jesus set out for a city called Nain, accompanied by his disciples and a great crowd of people. He was nearing the city gate, when a funeral came out. The dead man was his mother's only son; she was a widow, and was accompanied by a large number of the people of the city. When the Lord saw her, his heart was touched with pity for her and he said to her: 'Do not weep.' Then he went up and touched the bier. The bearers stopped, and Jesus said: 'Young man, I bid you, rise up.' The dead man sat up and began to speak, and Jesus gave him to his mother. All were seized with awe and praised God: 'A great prophet,' they said, 'has risen among us, and God has visited his people.' This description of him spread throughout Judea and the neighbouring country. (Lk 7:11-17)

John the Baptist consults Jesus from prison

When John heard news of all this from his disciples, he called two of them and sent them to the Lord to ask him, 'Are you the One who is to come, or should we wait for someone else?' The messengers came to him and said: 'John the Baptist has sent us to ask you, "Are you the One who is to come, or should we wait for someone else?"' There and then he cured many people of their diseases and infirmities and evil spirits, and gave sight to many who were blind. Then he answered the messengers: 'Go and tell John what you have seen and heard: *the blind see, the lame walk, lepers are cleansed, the deaf hear, the dead come to life, the poor have the gospel preached to them;* yet blessed is he who finds no cause for offence in me.' (Lk 7:18-23)

60

**Jesus praises John
as the greatest
of the prophets**

When John's messengers had left, Jesus spoke to the people about John; he said to them: 'What did you go out into the desert to see? A reed shaken by the breeze? No, but what did you go out to see? A man wearing fine clothes? But those who wear costly clothes and live in luxury are to be found in palaces. Then what did you go out to see? A prophet? Yes, I tell you, and more than a prophet. This is the man of whom the Scripture says: *See, I am sending my angel ahead of you, to prepare your way before you.* I tell you, among the sons of womankind none is greater than John. Yet even the least in the kingdom of God is greater than he.'

After hearing him, all the common people and even the tax-gatherers confessed God's judgement just and received John's baptism. But the Pharisees and lawyers refused what God wanted of them and were not baptized by him.

'How shall I describe the men of this generation? What are they like? They are like children sitting in a market-place who call to one another and sing, "We piped to you and you did not dance; we sang you a dirge and you did not mourn." John the Baptist comes neither eating bread nor drinking wine, and you say, "He is possessed by a devil"; the Son of Man comes eating and drinking, and you say, "Look! A glutton and a drunkard, a crony of tax-gatherers and sinners!" But Wisdom is justified by all her own children.'   (Lk 7:24-35)

**The woman who was
a sinner forgiven
in Simon the Pharisee's
house**

One of the Pharisees invited Jesus to a meal. So Jesus went into his house and took his place on one of the couches. A woman who had been leading a sinful life in the town heard that he was a guest in the Pharisee's house, and came with an alabaster vessel of myrrh, and placed herself behind the couch, near Jesus' feet. She was weeping, and began to bathe his feet with her tears and wipe them with her hair; then she kissed his feet and anointed them with the myrrh. The Pharisee who had invited him saw this and said to himself: 'If this man were a prophet, he would know that the woman who is touching him is a woman of evil life.' Jesus said to him: 'Simon, I have something to say to you.' 'Speak on, Master,' he said. Jesus said: 'A man had two debtors; one owed him five hundred silver pieces, and the other fifty. As they were unable to pay, he cancelled both debts. Tell me, which of them will love him more?' Simon replied: 'I suppose, the man who had the larger debt

62

cancelled.' Jesus said: 'You have judged rightly.' Then he turned towards the woman and said to Simon: 'You see this woman? I came into your house: you did not rinse my feet with water; she has bathed my feet with tears and wiped them with her hair. You gave me no kiss; she has not stopped kissing my feet since the moment I came in. You did not pour oil on my head; she has anointed my feet with myrrh. So I tell you, if she has shown much love, it is because her many sins have been forgiven; one who is forgiven little, shows little love.' Then he said to her: 'Your sins are forgiven.' At this his fellow-guests said to one another: 'Who is this who goes so far as to forgive sins?' But he said to the woman: 'Your faith has saved you; go in peace.'   (Lk 7:36-50)

Jesus and the devil. Sin against the Holy Spirit

Then he went into a house, and again such a crowd gathered that they could not even take a meal. When his own relations heard of it, they came out to restrain him; for people were saying that he was out of his mind. But the scribes who had come down from Jerusalem said: 'He has Beelzebul in him, and it is through the prince of devils that he casts out devils.' So he called them to him and spoke to them in parables: 'How can Satan cast out Satan? If a kingdom is at war with itself, it cannot last; if a household is at variance with itself, it will not be able to last; and if Satan has rebelled against himself and is at war with himself, he cannot last either — it is all over with him. When anyone enters a strong man's house to steal his goods, he can plunder the house only if he first ties up the strong man.

'I tell you truly, everything else will be forgiven the sons of men —their sins and all other blasphemies they may utter; but if anyone blasphemes against the Holy Spirit, he is never forgiven, but is liable to eternal damnation.' This, because they were saying: 'He has an unclean spirit.'
(Mk 3:20-30)

The true greatness of Jesus' mother and brothers

When his mother and his brothers arrived, they stood outside and sent word to him, to call him out. A large crowd was sitting round him, and they said to him: 'Look! Your mother and your brothers are outside, asking for you.' Jesus replied: 'Who is my mother? And who are my brothers?' Then he looked at the circle of those sitting round him, and said: 'Here are my mother and my brothers! Whoever does the will of God is brother and sister and mother to me.'
(Mk 3:31-35)

63

On that day Jesus went out of doors and sat down by the seaside. Such a throng gathered about him, that he went aboard a boat and sat down there, while all the people stood on the shore. Then he told them many things in parables. He said:

'A sower went out to sow. As he sowed, some of the seed fell by the wayside, and the birds of the air came and ate it. Some fell on rocky ground, where it had not much soil, and it sprouted at once, because it had not sunk deep but when the sun rose it was dried up, and as it had no roots, it withered. Some fell among briars, and the briars grew up and choked it. But the rest fell into good soil, and yielded a crop, some of it a hundred-fold, some sixty, some thirty. Let him hear who has ears to hear with.'

His disciples came to him and asked: 'Why do you speak to them in parables?'' He answered: ''To you it has been given to understand the mysteries of the kingdom of heaven; it has not been given to them. To the man who has plenty more will be given, and given in plenty; while the man who has little, will lose even what he has. The reason why I speak to them in parables is that though they look, they do not see, and though they listen, they neither hear nor understand. In them is fulfilled the prophecy of Isaiah which says:

However much you hear, you will not understand;
however much you look, you will not see;
for this people's heart is gross,
their ears are hard of hearing,
and they keep their eyes close,
for fear they should see with their eyes,
and hear with their ears,
and understand in their heart and repent,
and I should cure them.

'But as for you, blessed are your eyes, because they see, and your ears, because they hear. I tell you truly, many prophets and just men longed to see the things that you are seeing, and did not see them, and to hear the things that you are hearing, and did not hear them.

'Listen, then, while I explain the parable of the sower. When a man hears the word of the kingdom and fails to understand it, the evil one comes and snatches away what was sown in his heart. This is the meaning of the seed sown by the wayside. The seed sown on rocky ground stands for the man who hears the word and at once receives it with joy, but it does not take root in him, and does not last; when affliction or persecution comes because of the word, he falls away at once.

'The seed sown among briars means the man who hears the word, but worldly cares and the attractions of wealth choke it, and render it fruitless. The seed sown in good soil means those who hear the word and understand it, and yield a crop, some a hundred-fold, some sixty, and others thirty.'

(Mt 13:1-23)

Weeds: good and bad grow together: God's patience

Another parable too he set before them: 'The kingdom of heaven,' he said, 'is like this. A man sowed good seed in his field, but while everyone was asleep, an enemy of his came and over-sowed weeds among the wheat, and made off. As the blade came up and the ear filled out, the weed showed itself as well. So the servants went to the owner and said: "Sir, you sowed good seed in your field, did you not? How then does it come to have weeds in it?" He answered: "Some enemy has done this." The servants asked him: "Do you want us to go out and collect the weeds?" But he said: "No. In collecting the weeds you might root up the wheat as well. Let both grow together till the harvest. At harvest-time I shall tell the reapers to collect the weed first, and tie it in bundles for burning, and then gather the wheat into my barn."'

(Mt 13:24-30)

Mustard-seed and leaven: the good grows and ferments

Another parable too he set before them: 'The kingdom of heaven,' he said, 'is like mustard-seed, which a man takes and plants in his field. Of all seeds it is the smallest; but when it has grown up, it is larger than any garden plant and becomes a tree, so that the birds of the air can come and make a home in its branches.'

Another parable he told them was this: 'The kingdom of heaven is like leaven, which a woman takes and covers over with three measures of flour until the whole is leavened.'

All these things Jesus taught the people in parables, and he never spoke without a parable.

Thus was fulfilled the word spoken by the prophet when he said: *I shall speak in parables: I shall utter things kept secret since the foundation of the world.*

Then Jesus sent the crowds away and went indoors. His disciples came to him and said: 'Explain to us the parable of the weeds in the field.' Jesus answered: 'The sower of good seed is the Son of Man, the field is the world, the good seed stands for the children of the kingdom, the weeds are the children of the evil one. The enemy who sowed them is the devil, the harvest is the end of the world, and the reapers are the angels. Just as the weeds are collected and destroyed in the fire, so it will be at the end of the world. The Son of Man will send out his angels, and they will collect from his kingdom all who give offence and do what is evil, and they will throw them into the blazing furnace, where there will be weeping and gnashing of teeth. Then the just will shine out like the sun in the kingdom of their Father. Let him hear who has ears to hear with.'

(Mt 13:31-43)

The hidden treasure: everything is to be sacrificed for the kingdom of God

'The kingdom of heaven is like a treasure hidden in a field. A man finds it and covers it up, and then joyfully goes and sells all that he owns and buys the field

'Again, the kingdom of heaven is like a merchant in search of fine pearls. He finds one pearl of great value, and goes and sells all that he has and buys it.'

(Mt 13:44-46)

The net: only at the end will good and bad be separated

'Again, the kingdom of heaven is like a net which is cast into the sea and catches all kinds of fish. When it is full, the fishermen haul it up on the beach, and sit down and separate the good fish into pails, and throw away the worthless ones. So it will be at the end of the world: the angels will go out and separate the wicked from among the just, and throw them into the blazing furnace, where there will be weeping and gnashing of teeth.

'Have you understood all these parables?' They answered him: 'Yes.' He said to them: 'Then here is another: he who is both learned in the Scriptures and instructed in the kingdom of heaven is like a householder who brings out from his store-house things both new and old.'

(Mt 13:47-52)

MIRACLES OF CHRIST'S POWER

Jesus masters nature and stills the storm

That day, late in the evening, he said to them: 'Let us go over to the other side.' So they left the people and took him with them, just as he was, in the boat; and other boats accompanied him. Soon a great squall of wind arose, the waves were breaking over the boat, and it was already filling. Jesus was asleep on a cushion, in the stern. They awakened him, shouting: 'Master, don't you care? We are sinking!' He stood up, rebuked the wind, and said to the sea: 'Silence! Be still!' Then the wind fell, and there was a great calm. He said to them: 'Why are you so faint-hearted? Are you still without faith?' They were greatly over-awed, and said to one another: 'Who can this be, when even the wind and the sea obey him?'   (Mk 4:35-41)

The demoniac of Gerasa: Jesus masters evil spirits

So they came to the other side of the sea, to the country of the Gerasenes. When Jesus left the boat, a man possessed by an unclean spirit came out to meet him from among the tombs where he was living. Even with a chain no one could keep him in restraint any longer; many a time he had been bound with fetters and chains, but he had snapped the chains and smashed the fetters; and no one was able to tame him. Night and day, he was always among the tombs and on the mountains, howling and gashing himself with stones. When he saw Jesus in the distance, he ran and threw himself down before him and cried out in a loud voice: 'What have you to do with me, Jesus, Son of the Most High God? For God's sake, I adjure you, do not torment me!' (He said this because Jesus was already saying to him: 'Unclean spirit, go out of this man!') Jesus asked him: 'What is your name?' The reply came: 'Legion is the name, for there are many of us;' and the devils earnestly begged Jesus not to send them out of that territory. A great herd of pigs was grazing there on the mountainside; and the devils begged him: 'Let us go among the pigs and enter them.' Jesus gave them leave. So the

unclean spirits came out and entered the herd; but the pigs rushed down the slope into the sea (they were about two thousand in number), and were drowned in the water. The swineherds fled and told their story in the town and in the countryside, and people came to see what had happened. When they came to Jesus, they saw the man who had been possessed by the legion of devils sitting down, clothed and in his right mind; and they were struck with fear. Those who had seen it, explained to them what had happened to the possessed man, and told the story of the pigs. Then they asked Jesus to leave their country.

As he was going on board the boat, the man who had been possessed begged to be allowed to accompany him. But Jesus did not allow it. 'Go home to your own people,' he said, 'and tell them all that the Lord has done for you, and how he took pity on you.' So the man went off and began to proclaim in the Decapolis what Jesus had done for him; and all were filled with wonder. (Mk 5:1-20)

Jesus masters physical ill and cures the woman with haemorrhage

As soon as Jesus crossed back in the boat to the other side, a great crowd gathered to meet him. He was still on the shore, when the president of one of the synagogues came to him. Jairus was his name. He fell at Jesus' feet when he saw him, and earnestly begged his help: 'My little daughter is at the point of death,' he said, 'come and lay your hands on her, and you will save her life.' So Jesus went away with him, accompanied by great crowds which pressed about him.

Now there was a woman who had suffered from haemorrhages for twelve years, and had endured much at the hands of many doctors, and spent all she had without becoming any the better but rather worse. As she had heard about Jesus, she came up behind him in the crowd and touched his cloak, thinking to herself, 'If I touch even his clothes, I shall be healed.' At once the source of the haemorrhages was dried up, and she felt in her body that she was cured of her complaint. Jesus knew at once that power had gone out from him, and he turned round in the crowd and said: 'Who touched my clothes?' His disciples said: 'With the crowds as you see pressing round you, how can you ask, "Who touched me?"' Jesus was looking round to see who had done it. But the woman, who was in fear and trembling because she knew what had happened to her, came and fell at his feet and told him the whole truth. He said to her: 'Daughter, your faith has cured you. Go in peace, and you will remain free from your complaint.' (Mk 5:21-34)

Jesus masters death and raises Jairus' daughter

While he was still speaking, a message came from the house of the president of the synagogue: 'Your daughter is dead; why trouble the Master any more?' But Jesus overheard the message and said to the president: 'Do not be timid; only have faith!' He allowed no one to accompany him except Peter and James, and John the brother of James. When they reached the president's house, he found a noisy crowd of people wailing and lamenting loudly. So, as he went in, he said to them: 'What is the reason for this noise and lamentation? The child is not dead, she is only asleep.' They laughed at him; but after he had sent them all away, he took the child's father and mother and his own companions, and went into the room where the child lay sick. He took her by the hand and said to her: 'Talitha, koum', which means 'Little girl, (I bid you) rise up!' At once the girl rose up and began to walk about (she was twelve years old), and the people were beside themselves with amazement. Jesus strictly charged them that no one was to know of it, and he told them to give her something to eat. (Mk 5:35-43)

The miracles show that Jesus is the Messiah, but the Pharisees do not understand

As Jesus was passing on from there, two blind men went after him, shouting and crying: 'Have pity on us, Son of David!' Jesus entered a house, and the blind men came to him. He said to them: 'Do you believe that I can do it?' They answered: 'Yes, Lord.' Then he touched their eyes and said: 'As you have believed, so be it done for you!' And their eyes were opened. Jesus laid strict charge upon them: 'See that no one hears of this!' But they went away and spread his praises throughout the country.

As they were going away, a possessed man who was deaf and dumb was brought to Jesus. After the devil had been expelled, the dumb man spoke. The people were filled with wonder and said: 'Nothing like this has ever appeared in Israel!' But the Pharisees said: 'It is by the power of the prince of devils that he expels devils.' (Mt 9:27-34)

MISSION AND CRISIS IN GALILEE

Jesus sends out the apostles

Jesus went round all the towns and villages, teaching in the synagogues, proclaiming the good news of the kingdom, and curing every disease and every illness.

His heart was touched with pity for the people whom he saw, for they were harassed and worried, like *sheep without a shepherd*.

Then he said to his disciples: 'The harvest is abundant, but the labourers are few; you must pray to the Lord who owns the harvest to send labourers to reap his harvest.'

He called together his twelve disciples, and gave them power to drive out unclean spirits, and to cure every disease and every illness. These twelve Jesus sent out to preach; but first he gave them these instructions:

'Do not go to the Gentiles, and do not enter any city of the Samaritans; go rather to the lost sheep of the house of Israel.

'Go and proclaim that the kingdom of heaven is near. Cure the sick, raise the dead, cleanse lepers, drive out devils. What you have received as a gift, give as a gift. Get no gold or silver or copper for your purse; no knapsack for the journey; no second coat; no sandals or a staff; for the labourer has a right to his keep.' (Mt 9:35-37; 10:1; 10:5-10)

Jesus does not promise triumphs in this world but persecutions

'I am sending you out like sheep among wolves. Therefore be as wary as snakes, but innocent as doves. Be on your guard against men; they will bring you before their sanhedrins, and have you scourged in their synagogues. You will be brought before governors and kings because of me, to bear witness before them and before the Gentiles. When they deliver you up for trial, do not be anxious about what to say or how to say it. What you are to say will be made known to you at the time, for it is not you who will be speaking; the Spirit of your Father will be speaking through you.

'Do not fear them. There is nothing concealed that will not be revealed, nothing hidden that will not be made known. What I tell you in darkness, speak in the daylight; what you have heard in whispers, shout from the house-tops. Do not fear those who kill the body, but cannot kill the soul; fear rather the One who can ruin both soul and body in hell. Do not sparrows sell two for a penny? And yet not one of them will fall to the ground but by your Father's will. As for you, the very hairs of your head are all counted. Have no fear, then; for you are worth more than many sparrows.

'Everyone who acknowledges me before men, I shall acknowledge before my Father in heaven; and anyone who disowns me before men, I shall disown before my Father in heaven.' (Mt 10:16-20; 10:26-33)

Whoever helps an apostle will have the same reward as an apostle

'He who welcomes you, welcomes me; and he who welcomes me, welcomes him who sent me. He who welcomes a prophet because he is a prophet, will receive a prophet's reward; and he who welcomes a just man because he is a just man, will receive a just man's reward. And whoever gives one of these little ones a cup of cold water because he is a disciple, I tell you truly, he will not go unrewarded.'

(Mt 10:40-42)

Returning to Nazareth, Jesus is despised for his humble birth

He came to Nazareth, where he had been brought up, and on the sabbath day, as was his custom, he went to the synagogue. He stood up to read, and was given the scroll of the prophet Isaiah. Unrolling it, he found the passage which says:

The Spirit of the Lord is upon me,
for he has anointed me;
he has sent me to preach to the poor,
to proclaim release for prisoners
and sight for the blind,
to set free the oppressed,
and to proclaim the year of the Lord's favour.

Then he folded up the scroll, returned it to the minister, and sat down; and the eyes of all in the synagogue were fixed upon him. He began to speak to them: 'Today,' he said, 'with your own ears you are hearing that Scripture fulfilled.'

They all showed their approval of him and were full of wonder at the words of grace that came from his mouth, for they were thinking: 'Is not this Joseph's son?' Then he said to them: 'No doubt you will quote me the proverb, "Physician, heal yourself" — do here in your own country all that we have heard you did at Capernaum.' But he said: 'I tell you truly, no prophet is welcome in his own country.

'I assure you, there were many widows in Israel in the days of Elijah, when for three years and six months heaven sent no rain and famine gripped the whole land; yet it was not to any of them that Elijah was sent, but to a widow woman at Zarephat in the region of Sidon. And there were many lepers in Israel in the days of the prophet Elisha, and not one of them was cured, but only the Syrian Naaman.' At these words, everyone in the synagogue was filled with anger; they rose up and hurried him out of the town, and took him up to the brow of the hill on which their town was built, meaning to throw him over the cliff. But he passed through the middle of them and went his way. (Lk 4:16-30)

Herod Antipas has John the Baptist killed

When king Herod heard of Jesus, whose name was now becoming well known, his comment was: 'John the Baptist is risen from the dead! That is why these miraculous powers are at work in him.' Others were saying: 'He is Elijah,' and others: 'He is a prophet, like one of the prophets of old.' But when Herod heard of him he said: 'It is John, whom I beheaded! He has risen from the dead!'

For Herod himself had sent and arrested John and chained him in prison at the instigation of Herodias, the wife of his brother Philip, whom he had married. As John had constantly told Herod that it was not lawful for him to have his brother's wife, Herodias nursed enmity against John and wanted him put to death, but she could not bring this about because Herod protected John, recognising him to be a just and holy man; and after hearing him — which he used to do with pleasure — he was always greatly perplexed. However, an opportunity presented itself when Herod on his birthday gave a banquet for his grandees and officers and the leading men of Galilee. The daughter of Herodias came in and danced, and pleased Herod and his guests so much that the king said to the girl: 'Ask me for anything you like and I will give it to you!' In fact he swore an oath to her: 'Anything you ask of me I will give you, up to half of my kingdom.' She went out and said to her mother: 'What am I to ask for?' She said: 'The head of John the Baptist.' At once the girl hurried in to the king and made her request: 'I want you to give me here and now on a dish the head of John the Baptist.' The king was deeply grieved, but because of his oath and the presence of his guests he did not choose to rebuff her. He at once sent one of his bodyguards with orders to bring the head. The man went off and beheaded John in the prison, and brought his head on a dish and gave it to the girl, who gave it to her mother. When John's disciples heard this, they came and took away his body and laid it in a tomb. (Mk 6:14-29)

THE SECOND PASSOVER

Jesus multiplies the bread, as Moses had obtained manna in the wilderness

The apostles came back and rejoined Jesus and told him about what they had done and taught. Then he said to them: 'Come away by yourselves to some lonely place and rest a while.' (For there were so many people coming and going, that they had not even time to eat.) So they set out by themselves in the boat making for a deserted place. But many people saw them going and understood, and hastened to the place on foot from all the towns, and arrived before them. So when Jesus landed, he found a great crowd awaiting him; and his heart was touched with pity for them, because they were like *sheep without a shepherd*; and he preached to them at great length.

Then Jesus went up the mountain-side and sat down there with his disciples. (This was shortly before the Jewish feast of the Passover.) Raising his eyes, he saw that a large crowd was coming towards him; so he asked Philip: 'Where can we buy bread so that these people can have a meal?' (This was said to test Philip; Jesus himself knew what he would do.) 'Two hundred silver pieces would not buy enough bread for everyone to have even a little.' Then another of his disciples, Andrew, the brother of Simon Peter, said to him: 'There is a boy here who has five barley loaves and two small fishes; but they would not go far among all these people, would they? As the ground was covered with grass, Jesus said: 'Make the people sit down.' So they sat down; the men were about five thousand in number. Then Jesus took the loaves, offered a prayer of thanksgiving and distributed the bread to the guests; so too with the fishes. And he gave them as much as they wished. When they had eaten all they wanted, he said to his disciples: 'Gather up the pieces that remain over, so that nothing will be wasted.' They gathered them up and loaded twelve baskets with the pieces which remained over from the five loaves of barley bread after the meal. When the people saw the sign that Jesus performed, they declared: 'This is in truth the Prophet who was to come into the world.' But Jesus perceived that they meant to come and seize him to make him king. So he withdrew up the mountain by himself.

(Mk 6:30-34; Jn 6:3-15)

78

Then Peter
besought him
saying: 'Lord,
if it is you,
bid me come to you
on the water.'
He said: 'Come'

Jesus walks on the lake and Peter with him

Immediately afterwards he made his disciples go aboard the boat and sail ahead of him to the other side, while he himself was dismissing the people. This he did, and then went up by himself on the mountain-side to pray. When it was late, he was there alone, and the boat was now a long way out of land, toiling through the waves, for the wind was against them. Between three and six in the morning Jesus came towards them, walking on the water. When the disciples saw him doing this, they were filled with alarm, thinking it was a ghost, and they cried out in terror. But Jesus at once spoke to them: 'Courage! It is myself. Do not be afraid.'

Peter replied: 'Lord, if it is you, bid me to come to you on the water.' He said: 'Come.' Then Peter stepped out of the boat and walked on the water towards Jesus. But when he felt the force of the wind, he was frightened and began to sink. So he cried out: 'Lord, save me!' At once Jesus stretched out his hand and took hold of him; and he said to him: 'How little faith you have! Why did you doubt?' They boarded the boat, and the wind fell. Then the men in the boat worshipped Jesus exclaiming: 'You are indeed God's Son!'

(Mt 14:22-33)

Jesus cures the sick at Gennesaret

They reached the other side and landed at Gennesaret. The people there recognised Jesus, and sent word to all the neighbourhood, and they brought to him all the sick, and begged him to let them touch even the hem of his cloak; and all who did so were cured.

(Mt 14:34-36)

Eucharistic discourse: Jesus is the bread of life; the ancient manna did not save from death

The next day, the people were still on the far side of the sea. They knew that only the one boat had been there, that Jesus had not boarded it with his disciples, and that they had gone away without him. Other boats, however, had come from Tiberias and beached near where they had eaten the bread which the Lord had blessed. So when the people saw that neither Jesus was there nor his disciples, they boarded the boats and came to Capernaum to look for him. When they found him on the other side of the sea, they said to him: 'Rabbi, when did you come here?'

Jesus replied: 'I tell you truly, you are looking for me, not because you have seen signs, but because you ate the bread and were satisfied. You should work, not for the food that perishes, but for the food which remains and gives eternal life, the food which the Son of Man will give you; for God, his Father, has set his seal upon him.' So they asked him: 'What must we do, to carry out the works that God requires of us?' Jesus replied: 'The one work which God requires of you is this: you must believe in him whom God has sent.' They said to him: 'Then what sign do

you offer for us to see, so that we can believe in you? What is the work that you do? Our forefathers ate manna in the desert, as the Scripture says: *He gave them bread from heaven to eat.*' Jesus replied: 'I tell you truly, Moses did not give you the true bread from heaven, but my Father is offering it to you now. For the bread of God is the bread that comes down from heaven and gives life to the world.' They said to him: 'Lord, give us always this bread.'

Jesus said to them: ' I am the bread that gives Life. He who comes to me will never hunger, and he who believes in me will never thirst again. I tell you truly, the man who believes — he it is who has eternal life.

'I am the bread that gives life. Your forefathers ate manna in the desert, and they died. But here is bread coming down from heaven; such that if a man eats of it, he will not die. I am the living bread come down from heaven; eat this bread and you will live for ever. What is more, the bread that I shall give you is my own flesh, offered for the life of the world.'

Then the Jews began to dispute among themselves: 'How can he give us his flesh to eat?' they asked.

Jesus said to them: 'I tell you truly, if you do not eat the flesh of the Son of Man and drink his blood, you have not life in you. He who eats my flesh and drinks my blood has eternal life, and I shall raise him up at the last day. For my flesh is the true food, and my blood is the true drink. He who eats my flesh and drinks my blood abides in me, and I in him. As I am sent by the living Father and draw my life from the Father, so whoever eats me will draw his life from me. Here is the true bread that has come down from heaven! Your forefathers ate bread from heaven, and they died; but with this it is different: whoever eats this bread will live for ever.'

(Jn 6:22-58)

Only the twelve apostles understand Jesus' discourse and stay with him

Many of his disciples after hearing this said: 'This is a hard word he has said; who can accept it?'

Jesus knew in his heart that his disciples were murmuring about it; so he said to them: 'Does this overthrow your faith? But what if you see the Son of Man ascending to the place where he was before? That which is spirit gives life, that which is flesh is of no avail; the words that I have spoken are spirit and they give life. But there are some of you who do not believe.' (For Jesus knew from the beginning who were without faith, and who it was that would betray him.) He added: 'That is why I have told you that no one can come to me, unless it is granted him by the Father.'

After this, many of his disciples fell away and accompanied him no longer. Jesus therefore said to the Twelve: 'Do you also wish to go?' Simon Peter answered: 'Lord, to whom shall we go? You have the words that give eternal life: we have believed and we know that you are the Holy One of God.'

(Jn 6:60-70)

THE FEAST OF PENTECOST

Cure of a paralytic during the sabbath rest

Later there was a Jewish feast and Jesus went up to Jerusalem. Near the Sheep Gate in Jerusalem there is a pool with five porticoes, called in Hebrew "Bethzatha". A great many sick people lay under its porticoes, the blind, the lame, and the consumptive, waiting for a disturbance of the water (for from time to time an angel of the Lord used to come down to the pool and stir up the water; and the first to enter the pool after the disturbance was cured of whatever disease afflicted him). Among them was a man who had been crippled by illness for thirty-eight years. Jesus saw him lying there and knew that he had been ill a long time; so he said to him: 'Do you want to be cured?' The sick man replied: 'Sir, I have no one to put me in the pool when the water is disturbed; and while I am making my own way, someone else goes down before me.' Jesus said to him: 'Arise, pick up your stretcher, and walk!' At once the man was cured, and he picked up his stretcher and began to walk.

However, it was the sabbath day. So the Jews said to the man who had been cured: 'It is the sabbath, and it is not lawful for you to pick up your stretcher.' He replied: 'But the man who cured me said to me, "Pick up your stretcher and walk"!' So they asked him: "Who is this person who said to you, "Pick up your stretcher and walk"?' But the man who had been cured did not know who it was; for Jesus had gone away, as the place was crowded. Afterwards, Jesus came upon him in the temple, and said to him: 'Now that you have been cured, sin no more, or something worse may happen to you.' The man went off and informed the Jews that it was Jesus who had cured him.

It was for deeds like this, which Jesus did on the sabbath, that the Jews began to persecute him. But he replied by saying: 'My Father is always at work, and so too am I.' Then the Jews were all the more determined to kill him, because, besides breaking the law of the sabbath, he was calling God his own Father, and making himself equal to God. (Jn 5:1-18)

Jesus cures the daughter of a believing woman in Gentile country

After this, Jesus withdrew into the district of Tyre and Sidon. He did not wish anyone to know the house where he was staying, but he could not keep his presence secret.

Soon a Gentile woman — a Syrophoenician — whose little daughter had an unclean spirit, heard about him and came and threw herself at his feet, begging him to cast the devil out of her daughter. He said to her: 'Let the children be satisfied first; it is not right to take the children's bread and throw it to the dogs.' But she replied: 'True, Lord, but the dogs underneath the table may eat the scraps left by the children.' He said to her: 'For saying that — go home! The devil has gone out of your daughter.' She went home, and found the child lying on her bed, and the devil gone out of her. (Mt 7:24-30)

Cure of a deaf-mute and of a blind man with symbolic ritual acts

When Jesus left the territory of Tyre, he returned by way of Sidon to the sea of Galilee, through the middle of the territory of the Decapolis.

They brought a man who was deaf and had a speech impediment, and begged Jesus to lay his hands on him. Jesus took him aside from the crowd, put his fingers into the man's ears, and spat on his fingers and touched the man's tongue. Then, looking up to heaven, he sighed deeply and said to him: 'Ephphatha!' (which means 'Be opened!') At once the man's ears were opened and the impediment of his tongue was resolved and he began to speak normally. Jesus charged them not to tell anyone about it; but the more he charged them, the more freely they made it known. Their astonishment was unbounded, and they said: 'Everything he has done is wonderful! He makes the deaf hear and the dumb speak!'

When they reached Bethsaida, the people brought a blind man to Jesus and begged that he would touch him. Jesus took the blind man by the hand and led him out of the village. Then he spat on his eyes, laid his hands on him, and asked: 'Do you see anything?' The man began to recover his sight, and cried out: 'I see men! They look to me like trees, walking about!' Then Jesus laid his hands on the man's eyes once again, and he began to see clearly; his sight was restored, and he could see everything well. Then Jesus told him to go straight home without even entering the village.

(Mk 7:31-37; 8:22-26)

Jesus confers the primacy on Peter who recognises him as Messiah and Son of God

Jesus went also to the district of Caesarea Philippi. There he asked his disciples: 'Who do men say the Son of Man is?' They answered: 'Some say John the Baptist, others Elijah, others Jeremiah, or one of the prophets.' He said to them: 'And who do you say that I am?' Simon Peter answered: 'You are the Messiah, the Son of the Living God.'

Jesus replied: 'Simon bar Jonah, you are blessed indeed! For it was not flesh and blood that revealed this to you, but my Father in heaven. Now in my turn I say to you, You are Peter, The Rock, on which I shall build my Church, and the powers of hell will not prevail against it. To you I shall give the keys of the kingdom of heaven; what you bind on earth will be bound in heaven, and what you loose on earth will be loosed in heaven.'

Then he strictly forbade his disciples to tell anyone that he was the Messiah.

(Mt 16:13-20)

The transfiguration: Moses and Elijah confirm the way of the Cross

After six days, Jesus took Peter and James and John his brother, and led them up a high mountain alone; and he was transfigured before their eyes; his face shone like the sun, and his clothes were as bright as light. And Moses and Elijah appeared before them, conversing with Jesus. Then Peter cried out to Jesus: 'Lord, it is good for

us to be here! If you wish, I will make three tents here, one for you, one for Moses, and one for Elijah.' While he was still speaking, a bright cloud overshadowed them; and a voice spoke from the cloud: 'This is my beloved Son, in whom I am well pleased; listen to him!' When the disciples heard this, they fell on their faces and were stricken with fear. But Jesus came near and touched them, and said: 'Rise up, and do not be afraid.' Then they looked up and saw no one but Jesus alone. On their way down the mountain he strictly forbade them to tell anyone of the vision, until the Son of Man had been raised from the dead.

The disciples asked Jesus: 'Why then do the scribes say that Elijah must come first?' He answered: 'It is true that Scripture says, Elijah will come, and set all things in order; but I tell you Elijah has already come, and they did not recognise him, but ill-used him as they wished. And the Son of Man too is to suffer at their hands.' Then the disciples understood that he had been speaking of John the Baptist.   (Mt 17:1-13)

Jesus cures an epileptic boy whom the disciples cannot heal

As they came towards the other disciples, they saw that a great crowd had gathered round them, and some scribes were arguing with them. At the sight of Jesus, the whole crowd were struck with reverent awe and hastened to greet him. He asked them: 'What are you arguing about?' A man from the crowd replied: 'Master, I was bringing my son to you. He is possessed by a spirit that makes him dumb, and whenever it seizes him, it casts him down, and he foams at the mouth and gnashes his teeth, and goes rigid. I asked your disciples to cast it out, but they could not.' Jesus replied: 'O unbelieving generation, how long must I be with you, how long must I endure you? Bring him to me.' They brought the boy to him, and as soon as the spirit caught sight of Jesus, it threw the boy into convulsions, and he fell to the ground and rolled about foaming at the mouth. Jesus asked his father: 'How long has this been happening to him?' 'From childhood;' he replied, 'many a time it has thrown him into fire and water to take his life. But, if you can do anything, have pity on us and help us!' Jesus said to him: 'If, indeed! Everything is possible for one who believes.' At once the boy's father cried out: 'I do believe! Help my unbelief!' As Jesus saw that the crowd was becoming still larger, he spoke sternly to the unclean spirit: 'Deaf and dumb spirit,' he said, 'I command you, go out of him and never enter him again!' It shrieked and threw the boy into convulsions, and then it went out of him, leaving him so like a corpse that most of the bystanders thought he was dead. But Jesus took his hand and raised him; and he stood up.

When Jesus had come indoors, his disciples asked him privately: 'Why were we unable to cast it out?' He answered: 'This kind can be cast out only by prayer (and fasting).' (Mk 9:14-29)

Though Son of God, Jesus pays the tax for God's house

When they entered Capernaum, the collectors of the temple tax came to Peter and said: 'Does not your master pay the temple tax?' He answered: 'Why, yes!' When he entered the house, Jesus forestalled him by saying: 'What do you think, Simon? From whom do earthly kings collect taxes and tribute: From their own sons or from strangers?' Peter answered: 'From strangers,' and Jesus said to him: 'Yes, and so the sons are exempt. However, to avoid giving scandal, go down to the sea, throw in a hook, take the first fish that comes up, and when you open its mouth, you will find a silver coin inside. Take it and give it to them for the two of us.' (Mt 17:24-27)

Scandal is like death: better lose an eye ...

At that time the disciples came to Jesus, and asked: 'Who then is greatest in the kingdom of heaven?' Jesus called a little child to him and placed him in the middle of the disciples, and said: 'I tell you truly, if you do not become like children again, you will not enter the kingdom of heaven at all. He who humbles himself like this little child, is the greatest in the kingdom of heaven.

'Whoever receives one such child in my name receives me. But whoever scandalises one of these little ones who believe in me he would have been better off with a great millstone hung about his neck and sunk in the depths of the sea.

'Woe to the world because of its scandals! Come they must, yet woe to the man through whom scandal comes!

'If your hand or your foot scandalises you, chop it off and throw it away! It is better for you to enter life lame or crippled, than to keep your two hands and two feet but be thrown into everlasting fire.

'And if your eye scandalises you, out with it, throw it away! It is better for you to enter life with only one eye than to be thrown into hell fire with two.

'See that you do not despise any of these little ones: for I tell you, their guardian angels on high always look upon the face of my Father in heaven.' (Mt 18:1-10)

89

Brotherly correction, forgiveness of sins, and common prayer

'If your brother wrongs you, go and charge him with his fault privately between yourselves. If he listens to you, you will have gained a brother. If he does not, take one or two others with you, so that *everything said can be vouched for by the word of two or three witnesses*. If he disregards them too, report him to the church. And if he disregards even the church, then treat him as you would a heathen or a tax-gatherer. I tell you truly, whatever you bind upon earth shall be bound in heaven; and whatever you loose on earth shall be loosed in heaven. And again, I tell you truly, if any two of you on earth unite in making any petition, it will be granted by my Father in heaven.

'For where two or three are gathered together in my name, I am there in the midst of them.'

(Mt 18:15-20)

Parable of the two debtors: God cannot forgive those who are not themselves capable of forgiving

Then Peter came to him and said: 'Lord, how many times should I forgive my brother, if he goes on doing me wrong? As many as seven times?' Jesus replied: 'I tell you, not seven times, but seventy times seven. So the kingdom of heaven is like this. A king once wished to settle his accounts with his servants. When he began the reckoning, one man was brought to him who owed a million pounds. As he could not meet the debt, his master gave orders for him to be sold, with his wife and children and all his possessions, in order to make repayment. The servant fell down at his feet and said: "Give me time, and I will pay you the whole sum." The master's heart was touched with pity for his servant, and he let him go and remitted his debt.

'Then the servant went out and came upon one of his fellow-servants who owed him five pounds; seizing him by the throat he said: "Pay back what you owe!" His fellow-servant fell down and begged him: "Give me time, and I will repay you." But he refused; instead he went and threw him into prison until he should pay the debt. When the other servants saw what happened, they were greatly upset, and went and told their master the whole story. The master sent for the servant and said to him: "Wretched servant that you are! I remitted the whole of that great debt of yours, because you asked me. Ought you not to have pity on your fellow-servant, just as I had pity on you?" Then in his anger he handed him over to the torturers until he should pay his whole debt. That is how my heavenly Father will deal with you if brother does not forgive brother from his heart.'

(Mt 18:21-35)

THE FEAST OF TABERNACLES

Crisis about the mystery of Christ

After this, Jesus travelled about in Galilee; he did not wish to continue his journeys in Judea, because the Jews wanted to put him to death. Shortly before the Jewish feast of Tabernacles, his brethren said to him: 'Do not stay here; go into Judea and let your disciples see these works of yours that you are doing. Nobody who wants a thing publicly known does it in secret. If you are doing things like these, you should show yourself to the world.' For even his own brethren did not believe in him. Jesus said to them: 'My time has not yet come; for you every time is the right time. The world cannot hate you, but it hates me, because I testify that its works are evil. Go up to the feast yourselves, but I am not going up to this feast, because my appointed time has not yet come.' Having given them this answer, Jesus stayed in Galilee. But after his brethren had gone up to the feast, he too went up, not openly, but in secret.

Now the Jews were looking for him at the feast and asking where he was. Among the people there was much whispering about him; some said: 'He is a good man,' while others said: 'No! He is leading the people astray.' But no one spoke openly about him for fear of the Jews.

(Jn 7:1-13)

Necessity of making up one's mind about Jesus

Half way through the festival, Jesus went up to the temple and began to teach. The Jews were shocked, and said: 'How can this man know the Scriptures without having studied?' Jesus answered them: 'My teaching is not my own; it is the teaching of the one who sent me. Anyone who chooses to do the will of God will know whether this teaching is from God, or whether I am giving a doctrine of my own. A teacher who gives a doctrine of his own is seeking his own glory; but a teacher who seeks the glory of the one who sent him speaks the truth, and there is no deception in him.

'Moses gave you the Law, did he not? And yet none of you keeps the Law. Why do you want to put me to death?' The crowd answered: 'You are possessed! Who wants to put you to death?' Jesus replied: 'I have done one work, and you are all shocked. This was why Moses gave you the law of circumcision (not that it began with Moses; it goes back to the patriarchs) and you circumcise a man on the sabbath. If then a man receives circumcision on the sabbath, so that the Law of Moses shall not be broken, are you angry with me because I have cured a man's whole body on a sabbath? Cease to judge by outward appearances; judge by the standard of justice.'

By this time, some of the people of Jerusalem were saying: 'Is not this the man whom they want to put to death? And look! Here he is, speaking in public, and they say nothing to him! Perhaps our rulers have recognised that he is in truth the Messiah. And yet we know where this man comes from; but when the Messiah comes, nobody will know where he is from'. Jesus, therefore, cried out, while he was teaching in the temple: 'Do you know me? and do you know where I come from? I have come not of my own choice, but sent by one who is true. You do not know him; but I do know him, for I know that I come from him, and it is he who sent me.' The Jews wanted to arrest him for saying this; but nobody raised a hand against him, for his hour had not yet come.

Among the people, however, many believed in him. They said: 'When the Messiah comes, will he work more miracles than this man has done?'

When the Pharisees heard the murmur of this debate about him among the people, they and the chief priests sent guards to arrest him. Then Jesus said: 'I shall be with you still a little longer, then I am going to him who sent me; you will seek me and will not find me, for where I am, you cannot come.' The Jews said to one another: "Where does he mean to go, that we should not find him? Is he going to our people dispersed among the Greeks, and to teach the Greeks themselves? What does he mean by this saying of his: "You will look for me and will not find me; and where I shall be you cannot come"?'   (Jn 7:14-36)

93

Controversy about Jesus: wonder-working prophet or devil-possessed deceiver?

On the last, the greatest, day of the feast, Jesus stood up and cried out: 'If anyone is thirsty, let him come to me; let him drink, who believes in me; for the Scripture says, *From his heart will flow streams of living water.*' This he said of the Spirit which believers in him were to receive later; for as yet the Spirit was not given, because Jesus had not yet been glorified.

Some of the people, on hearing this, said: 'He is certainly the Prophet,' and some said: 'He is the Messiah.' But others said: 'Surely the Messiah is not to come from Galilee? Does not the Scripture say that *the Messiah is to come from the posterity of David, and from David's city of Bethlehem?*' So the people were in disagreement about him. Some of them wanted to arrest him; but no one raised his hands against him.

The guards returned to the chief priests and Pharisees, who asked: 'Why have you not brought him with you?' The guards replied: 'No man ever spoke like this before.' The Pharisees answered: 'Have you too been led astray? Has any of the rulers believed in him, or any of the Pharisees?' At this, one of their number, Nicodemus, who had once visited Jesus, spoke up: 'Does our Law condemn a man,' he asked, 'without first giving him a hearing and finding out what he is doing?' They replied: 'Are you too from Galilee? Study the Scriptures, and you will find that prophets never come from Galilee.'

Then they all went home, but Jesus went to the Mount of Olives.

(Jn 7:37-53)

The Messiah has come to save: Jesus pardons the adulterous woman

In the early morning he appeared again in the temple, and all the people gathered about him. He had sat down and begun to teach them, when the scribes and Pharisees brought a woman who had been taken in adultery, and made her stand before him in full view of everyone. 'Master,' they said, 'this woman has been taken in the act, committing adultery. In the Law, Moses laid down that we are to stone such a woman. What do you say about it?' They put this question to test him, in order to have a charge to bring against him. Jesus, however, had bent down and was writing on the ground with his finger. As they persisted in pressing the question, he looked up and said to them: 'Whoever is without sin among you can cast the first stone at her.' Then he bent down again and continued writing on the ground. When her accusers heard this, they went away, one by one, first the oldest and finally the youngest; and Jesus was left alone, with the woman still standing before him. Jesus looked up and said to her: 'Woman, where are they? Has no one condemned you?' She said: 'No, Lord.' Jesus replied: 'Nor do I condemn you. Go your way, and do not sin again.'

(Jn 8:1-11)

Sin is slavery: truth will set you free. God's name "I am" (Yahweh) is applied to Jesus

Jesus said to those of the Jews who had believed in him: 'If you remain faithful to my word, you are truly my disciples; you will know the truth, and the truth will set you free.' They replied: 'We are the descendants of Abraham and have never yet been slaves to anyone; what do you mean by saying that we shall be set free?' Jesus answered them: 'I tell you truly, everyone who commits sin is a slave of sin. [. . .] 'If you are Abraham's children, then follow the example of Abraham. Instead, you want to put me to death, a man who has revealed to you the truth, which I heard from God. Abraham did no such thing. But you are indeed following the example of your father.' They said to him: 'We were not born of adultery! We have one father, God alone.' Jesus answered: 'If God were your father, you would love me; for it is from God that I come forth, it is from God that I have come. I have not come of my own choice, but sent by him. Why do you not recognise my voice? It is because you cannot accept my word. The father from whom you are descended is the devil, and you are bent on carrying out your father's desire. He has been a murderer from the beginning. He does not take his stand on truth, because truth is not in him. [. . .] 'I tell you truly, if anyone keeps my word, he will never see death.' The Jews said to him: 'Now we are certain that you are possessed. Abraham died, and so did the prophets; and yet you say, "If anyone keeps my word, he will never taste death." Are you then greater than our father Abraham who died, and greater than the prophets who also died? What are you claiming to be?'

Jesus answered: 'If I glorify myself, my glory is nothing. It is my Father who glorifies me, he whom you call your God, though you do not know him. But I do know him, and if I were to say that I do not know him I should be a deceiver like you; but I do know him and I keep his word.

'Your father Abraham rejoiced that he should see my day; he saw it, and was glad.' The Jews said to him: 'You are not yet fifty years old, and you have seen Abraham?' Jesus answered: 'I tell you truly, before Abraham was, *I am.*' Then they picked up stones to hurl at him; but Jesus hid himself, and went out of the temple.   (Jn 8:31-59)

Jesus cures the man born blind, on the sabbath day

As Jesus went away, he saw a man who had been blind from birth. His disciples put to him the question: 'Rabbi, whose sin caused him to born blind, his own or his parents'?' Jesus replied: 'It is not that he or his parents sinned; he has been blind from birth in order that the way God works may be revealed in his life. We must do the works of him who sent me while daylight lasts. Night is coming, when no one can work. So long as I am in the world, I am the light of the world.'

With these words he spat on the ground and mixed the spittle into mud. Then he smeared the man's eyes with the mud, and said to him: 'Go and wash in the pool of Siloam.' ("Siloam" means "one who is sent".) The man went off and washed, and when he left the pool he could see.

His neighbours and those who had formerly known him by sight as a beggar said: 'Is not this the man who used to sit and beg?' Some said yes it was, and others said: 'No, it is just someone like him.' But he replied: 'Yes, I am the man.' So they said to him: 'Then how comes it that your eyes are open?' He replied: 'The man called Jesus mixed some mud and anointed my eyes and said to me, "Go to Siloam and wash." So I went and washed and I could see.' They said to him: 'Where is he?' He replied: 'I do not know.' Then they took him to the Pharisees, this man who had been blind.

Now the day on which Jesus had mixed the mud and opened his eyes was a sabbath. So the Pharisees asked him to repeat to them how it had come about that he could see. He replied: 'He put mud on my eyes, and I washed them, and now I can see.' Some of the Pharisees said: 'This man is not from God, because he does not observe the sabbath.' Others replied: 'But how can a sinner work miracles like these?' So there was a division of opinion among them. Then they questioned the blind man again: 'Since he has opened your eyes, what do you say about him?' He replied: 'I say that he is a prophet.'   (Jn 9:1-17)

The blind man sees: the obstinate Pharisees remain blind

The Jews, however, would not believe that he had been blind and had gained the use of his eyes, until they had summoned his parents and questioned them. 'Is this your son?' they asked. 'Do you affirm that he was born blind? If so, how comes it that he can now see?' His parents answered: 'We know that this is our son, and that he was born blind; but how comes that he can now see, we do not know. Nor do we know who opened his eyes. Ask him. He is of age, he will speak for himself.' His parents answered in this way because they were afraid of the Jews, who had already agreed that if anyone confessed Jesus as the Messiah, he should be excommunicated from the synagogue. That is why his parents said: 'He is of age; ask him.'

Once again the Pharisees summoned the man who had been blind. They said to him: 'Give glory to God! We know that this man is a sinner.' He answered: 'Whether he is a sinner, I do not know; but one thing I do know: that I was blind and now I can see.' They said to him: 'What did he do to you? How did he open your eyes?' He replied: 'I have told you already, and you would not listen to me; why do you want to hear my story again? Don't tell me that you want to become his disciples too!' Then they turned on him with scorn: 'You can be that fellow's disciple;'

they said, 'we are disciples of Moses. We know that God spoke to Moses; but as for him, we do not know where he comes from.' The man replied: 'Amazing! You do not know where he is from, and yet he has opened my eyes! We know that God does not hear the prayers of sinners, but does hear those who revere him and do his will. Opening the eyes of a man born blind — it is a thing unheard of in all past time. If this man were not from God, he would have no powers at all.' They replied: 'You were born steeped in sin, and do you presume to lecture us?' Then they cast him out.

When Jesus heard that they had cast him out, he looked for him and said to him: 'Do you believe in the Son of God?' He answered: 'Who is he, Lord? Tell me, so that I can believe in him.' Jesus said to him: 'It is someone you have seen — the person who is speaking to you.' He answered: 'I believe, Lord.' And he knelt down and adored him.

Then Jesus said: 'I have come into the world to carry out a judgement: the blind shall see and those who see shall become blind.' Some of the Pharisees who were with him heard this and said to him: 'Are we too blind?' Jesus replied: 'If you were blind, you would have no sin; as it is, you say, "We can see." Therefore your sin remains.'   (Jn 9:18-41)

The good Samaritan: you must be a "neighbour" to anyone you meet

Once a lawyer rose and put a question to test him; 'Master,' he asked, 'what must I do to gain eternal life?' Jesus replied: 'In the Law what is written? What do you read there?' He answered: *'Love the Lord your God with your whole heart, and with your whole soul, and with your whole strength,* and with your whole mind, *and your neighbour as yourself.'* Jesus said to him: 'You have answered rightly; do this and you will have life.'

The lawyer, however, wishing to justify himself, said to Jesus: 'But who is my "neighbour"?' Jesus gave him this answer: A man was on his way down from Jerusalem to Jericho when he fell into the hands of robbers, who stripped him and beat him, and went away leaving him half dead. A priest happened to be going down that way; he saw him and passed by. A levite too came along the road; he saw him and passed by. But a Samaritan on his travels came upon him, and when he saw him, his heart was touched with pity. He went over to him, treated his wounds with oil and wine and bound them up, then put him astride his own mount and brought him to an inn, and took care of him. Next day, he took out two silver pieces and gave them to the innkeeper. "Look after him," he said, "and anything that you spend over and above this, I will repay you when I come back." Now which of these three, do you think, proved himself a neighbour to the man who fell into the hands of the robbers?' He said: 'The one who showed him charity.' Jesus replied: 'Go and do as he did.'   (Lk 10:25-37)

'A Samaritan on
his travels came
upon him, and when
he saw him,
his heart was
touched with pity'

Martha and Mary: household chores and God's word

They journeyed on and entered a certain village, where a woman named Martha welcomed them into her house. She had a sister called Mary who sat down at the Lord's feet and listened to his teaching. Martha was distracted by her many household tasks. So she stopped and said: 'Lord, do you not care that my sister has left me to do all the work by myself? If you do, tell her to help me.' But the Lord said to her: 'Martha, Martha, you worry and fret over many things, but only one thing is necessary. Mary has chosen the best part, and it shall not be taken away from her.'

(Lk 10:38-42)

The importunate friend: prayer must be insistent

He added: 'Suppose one of you has a friend: He goes to the friend's house at midnight and says to him: "My friend, lend me three loaves; an acquaintance of mine has arrived on a journey, and I have nothing to set before him." The friend inside replies: "Do not be a nuisance; the door is locked; my children and myself are already in bed. I cannot get up to satisfy you." I tell you, even if friendship will not make him leave his bed to give him the loaves, in the end he will yield to importunity and rise up and give him what he wants.'

'I tell you: ask, and your request will be granted; seek, and you will find; knock, and the door will be opened to you. It is always he who asks that receives, and he who seeks that finds; and to him who knocks the door will be opened. Is there any father among you who will hand his son a stone when he asks for bread, or a snake when he asks for fish, or a scorpion when he asks for an egg? If then you, bad as you are, know how to give good things to your children, how much more will your heavenly Father give the Holy Spirit to those who ask him!'

(Lk 11:5-13)

Jesus, invited to dinner, condemns the empty formalism of the Pharisees

After Jesus had said this, a Pharisee asked him to dine with him. So he went in and took his place at table. The Pharisee was surprised to see that he did not wash before dinner. But the Lord said to him: 'You Pharisees are content to clean the outside of cup and plate, when inside you are lined with the proceeds of greed and extortion. Fools that you are! Did not he who made the outside make the inside too? Yet give as alms what is inside the cup, and then see how everything will be clean for you!'

'Woe to you Pharisees! You pay tithes on mint, rue and every herb, but you neglect justice and the love of God. These are the virtues you ought to have practised — while not neglecting those other things.

'Woe to you Pharisees! You love to have the first seats in the synagogues and to be bowed to in the market-places.

'Woe to you! You are like hidden tombs, which men walk over without noticing.'

One of the lawyers interposed. 'Master,' he said, 'in speaking like this, you insult us too.' Jesus said: 'Woe to you lawyers as well! You lay on men burdens that are hard to carry, but will not put one finger to those burdens yourselves.

'Woe to you who build monuments to the prophets whom your fathers killed! You do but testify that you approve your fathers' deeds: they killed the prophets, and you build tombs for them. That is why the Wisdom of God declared: "I shall send them prophets and apostles; some of them they will persecute and kill; then they will be called to answer for the blood of all the prophets shed since the beginning of the world, from the blood of Abel to the blood of Zechariah, who was slain between the altar and the sanctuary." Yes, I tell you, this generation will have to answer for it.

'Woe to you lawyers! You have taken possession of the key of knowledge, but you have not gone in yourselves, and have hindered those who want to enter.'

When Jesus left the place, the scribes and Pharisees began to attack him fiercely and assail him with questions on many things. They were watching to catch some word from his own lips to use against him.

(Lk 11:37-54)

Avarice makes people deaf to the needs of the soul

Someone from the crowd said to him: 'Master, tell my brother to give me my share of our inheritance.' Jesus replied: 'My friend, who set me up as judge or arbitrator between you?'
Then he said to the people: 'Be careful to avoid all greed; a man's life is not lengthened by amassing more wealth than he needs.' And he told them a parable: 'There was a rich man whose farm produced large crops. He thought to himself, "What am I to do? I have no room to store my crops." Then he said, "I know: I will pull down my barns and build larger ones and store all my grain and goods in them; then I shall say to myself, 'Now you have plenty of good things stored up for many a year; take your ease, eat, drink, and enjoy yourself'." But God said to him, "Foolish man! This very night your life is forfeit; and the goods you have amassed, whose will they be?" So it will be with the man who hoards for himself but has no riches in the sight of God.' (Lk 12:13-21)

**Jesus, the true
shepherd, gives his
life for the sheep**

'I tell you truly, a man who does not enter a sheepfold through the gate but by some other way is a thief and a robber. The man who enters through the gate is the shepherd to whom the sheep belong. The keeper opens the gate for him, and the sheep heed his voice; he calls his own sheep by name and leads them out. When he has brought all of them out, he goes ahead of them, and the sheep follow him, because they know his voice. But they will not follow a stranger; they run away from him, because they do not recognise the voices of strangers.' Jesus put this parable before them, but they did not understand what it was that he was telling them.

Then Jesus spoke to them again: 'I tell you truly, I am the gate for the sheep. All who came before me were thieves and robbers; but the sheep did not heed them. I am the gate; anyone who enters through the gate will be saved; he will pass in and out and find pasture. Thieves come only to steal and slaughter and destroy the sheep; I have come that they may have life and still more life.

'I am the good shepherd; a good shepherd lays down his life for his sheep. When a hired man sees a wolf coming, as he is not their shepherd and they are not his sheep, he leaves the sheep to be harried and scattered by the wolf, while he makes his escape. He is but a hired man and has no real concern for the sheep. I am the good shepherd; and I know my own and my own know me, just as the Father knows me and I know the Father; and I will lay down my life for the sheep.

'I have other sheep too, which are not of this fold; those too I must lead; they will heed my voice, and there will be one flock with one shepherd.

'The Father loves me for this, that I am willing to lay down my life, and afterwards to receive it back again. No one will wrest it from me; I shall lay it down of my own free will. It is in my power to lay it down, and it is in my power to receive it back again.'

(Jn 10:1-18)

**Jesus claims
to be God
like the Father**

Winter came, and the feast of Dedication was celebrated at Jerusalem. Jesus was in the temple, walking up and down in Solomon's colonnade, when the Jews gathered about him and said: 'How long are you going to keep up this suspense? If you are the Messiah, tell us so in plain words.'

Jesus answered: 'I have told you, but you do not believe it: the works which I do in my Father's name are my witnesses. But you do not believe me, and the reason is that you are not sheep of mine. My sheep hear my voice; I know them, and they follow me; I give them eternal life, and they will never perish. No one will wrest them out of my hand; my Father, who gave them to me, is greater than all; and no one can wrest them from the Father's hand. The Father and I are one.' At this, the Jews again took up stones, to stone him.

(Jn 10:22-31)

Jesus is not blaspheming when he claims to be God: his works show his divinity

Jesus said to them: 'At the Father's bidding, I have done many good works in your sight; for which of them do you mean to stone me?' The Jews replied: 'It is not for any good work that we mean to stone you, but for blasphemy, and because though a mere man, you declare yourself to be God.' Jesus answered: 'Does not the Scripture say, in that Law of yours: *I said, you are gods?* If you grant that Scripture calls "gods" those to whom God's word was addressed, and that Scripture cannot be set aside, are you accusing of blasphemy one whom the Father has sanctified and sent into the world, just because I have said, "I am God's Son"? If the works that I am doing are not the works of my Father, do not believe in me; but if they are, then even if you will not believe in me, believe in my works; they will make you know and understand that the Father is in me and I am in the Father.'

They tried again to arrest him, but he escaped from their hands and went away across the Jordan to the place where John had begun his baptizing. There he stayed, and many people came to him. 'John,' they said, 'worked no miracles; but everything that John said about this man was true.' And many believed in him there. (Jn 10:32-42)

THE LAST JOURNEY TO JERUSALEM

The unbelieving Jews and the call to the Gentiles

He was journeying on through towns and villages, teaching and making his way towards Jerusalem, when someone said to him: 'Lord, will only a few be saved?' He answered: 'The door is narrow; strive hard to get in; for many, I assure you, will try to enter and will fail.'

'Once the master of the house has decided to shut the door, you will stand outside knocking, and call out, "Lord, open the door for us!" but he will answer, "I do not know where you come from." Then you will say, "But we ate and drank with you, and you taught in our streets!" and he will say again, "I do not know where you come from; away from me, all you evil doers!" Then there will be weeping and gnashing of teeth, for you will see Abraham, Isaac and Jacob and all the prophets inside the kingdom of God, and while you yourselves are shut out, others will come from north, south, east and west and sit down to feast in the kingdom of God. Yes, those who are now last will be first, and those who are first will be last.'

At this time, some Pharisees came to him and said: 'You had better leave this place and go elsewhere, because Herod wants to put you to death.' He replied: 'Go and say to that fox, "Today and tomorrow I shall drive out devils and cure the sick, and on the third day I have finished." But to you Pharisees, I say, today, tomorrow and the next day I must go on my way; for a prophet cannot meet his death anywhere but in Jerusalem.'

'Jerusalem, Jerusalem, slayer of prophets, murderess of the messengers sent to you, how often have I longed to gather your children, as a hen gathers her brood under her wings, and you would not let me! *See then, your house is forsaken!* I tell you, you will not see me again until the day when you will cry, *Blessed is he who comes in the name of the Lord.*'

(Lk 13:22-35)

Following Jesus needs heroism and hard decisions

Large numbers of people were making the journey with him; and he turned and said to them: 'If anyone comes to me and does not hate his father and mother, and wife and children, and brother and sisters, and indeed his very self, he cannot be a disciple of mine. If you do not carry your cross and come after me, you cannot be a disciple of mine. Suppose one of you wants to build a tower: does he not first sit down and work out the cost, to see if he will have the means to finish? For if he lays the foundation and then cannot finish the work, all who see it will laugh at him and say, "This is the man who began to build and could not finish." Or if one king is about to march against another to meet him in battle, will he not first sit down and consider whether with his own ten thousand men he can face an enemy who has twenty thousand? If he decides not, he sends envoys while his enemy is still a long way off, and asks for terms of peace. So too with you: if anyone among you does not bid farewell to all his possessions, he cannot be my disciple.'

(Lk 14:25-33)

God loves the penitent. Parables of the lost sheep and the lost coin

All the tax-gatherers and sinners were drawing near to listen to him. This made the Pharisees and scribes murmur to one another: 'This man welcomes sinners and sits at table with them!' Jesus therefore told them this parable: 'If any of you has a hundred sheep and loses one of them, does he not leave the ninety-nine in the desert and go after the lost sheep until he finds it? And when he finds it, does he not put it on his shoulders joyfully, and come home and call his friends and neighbours together and say to them, "Rejoice with me, because I have found the sheep I had lost"? I tell you that in the same way there will be rejoicing in heaven over one sinner who repents rather than over ninety-nine just men who have no need of repentance.

'Or if a woman has ten silver coins and loses one, does she not light a lamp and sweep the house and search carefully until she finds it? And when she finds it does she not call her friends and neighbours together and say, "Rejoice with me, because I have found the coin I had lost"? In the same way, I tell you, there is rejoicing among the angels of God over one sinner who repents.'

(Lk 15:1-10)

The prodigal son:
one brother runs away
from home, the other
is dutiful but selfish

He went on: 'There was once a man who had two sons, and the younger of them said to his father: "Father, give me my share of the property." So his father divided the property for them. Not many days later, the younger son sold out his share, collected the money, and left home for a distant country. There he lived recklessly and squandered his money. When he had spent all he had, a severe famine came over that country, and he began to be in need. So he went and attached himself to one of the local nobility, who sent him to his farm to look after the pigs. He was glad even to fill his belly with the husks that the swine were eating; and no one gave him anything. Then he came to his senses and thought, "All those hired servants of my father's have more than they need to eat, and I sit here, dying of hunger! I will rise and go back to my father, and say to him, 'Father, I have sinned against heaven and before you; I no longer deserve to be called your son; treat me as one of your hired servants.'" So he rose and went to his father. But while he was still far off, his father saw him and was filled with pity for him, and ran and put his arms round his neck and kissed him. His son said to him: "Father I have sinned against heaven and before you; I no longer deserve to be called your son." But the father said to his servants: "Quick! Bring the richest robe and put it on him; put a ring on his finger, and sandals on his feet; bring the fatted calf and kill it, and let us eat and make merry, because this son of mine was dead and has come back to life, he was lost and now he is found." So they began to make merry.

'Meanwhile, the elder son was out in the fields. Coming back, as he approached the house, he heard music and dancing. So he called one of the servants and asked what it was all about. The servant replied: "Your brother has come home, and your father has killed the fatted calf because he has received him back safe and sound." The son was angry and would not go in. So his father came out and pleaded with him. But he replied: "Look! I have slaved for you all these years, and never disobeyed an order of yours; and you have never given me even a kid, to make merry with my friends. But this son of yours comes back after devouring your property with the aid of harlots, and you kill the fatted calf for him!" His father said to him: "My boy, you are always with me; everything I have is yours. But it was right to be glad and make merry, because your brother was dead and has come back to life, he was lost and now he is found."'

(Lk 15:11-32)

108

The unjust steward: we must be shrewd in spiritual matters

He also said to his disciples: 'There was once a man who received reports that his steward was wasting his property. He summoned the steward and said to him: "What is this I hear about you? Hand over the accounts of your stewardship, because you can remain steward no longer." The steward said to himself, "What am I going to do, now that my master is taking away the stewardship from me? I cannot dig, and I am ashamed to beg. I know what I shall do. I shall make sure that when I am removed from the stewardship, people will welcome me into their houses." So he summoned his master's debtors one by one. He said to the first, "How much do you owe my master?" and the man replied: "A thousand gallons of oil." The steward said to him: "Here is your account; sit down at once and make it five hundred." Then he asked another: "How much do you owe?" He answered: "A hundred bushels of wheat." The steward said to him: "Here is your account; make it eighty." And the master praised his dishonest steward for the shrewdness of his action; for in dealing with the generation to which they belong the sons of this world are shrewder than the sons of light.'

(Lk 16:1-8)

There can be no compromise between God and riches

'If a man is trustworthy in small matters, he can be trusted also in large; and if he is dishonest in small matters, he will be dishonest also in large.

'If you have not proved trustworthy about wordly wealth, who will trust you with true riches? And if you have not proved trustworthy in caring for the goods of others, who will give you any for yourselves?

'No servant can serve two masters; he will either hate one and love the other, or be loyal to one and despise the other. You cannot serve both God and Money.'

The Pharisees, who were avaricious men, heard all this and sneered at Jesus. But he said to them: 'You are the sort who pass themselves off as just in the eyes of men; but God knows your hearts. What men look up to is an abomination in the eyes of God.'

(Lk 16:10-15)

Dives and Lazarus: wealth encourages selfishness

'There was once a rich man, who dressed in purple and fine linen and dined in state every day. At his gate lay a poor man named Lazarus, who longed to satisfy his hunger with the scraps from the rich man's table. He was infested with sores, and the dogs would come and lick them. One day this poor man died and was carried by angels to Abraham's bosom. The rich man also died and was buried. Suffering torment in hell, he lifted up his eyes and saw Abraham far

110

away, with Lazarus in his bosom. He cried out: "Father Abraham, have mercy on me! Send Lazarus to dip the tip of his finger in water and cool my tongue, for I am tormented in these flames." But Abraham said: "My child, remember that you had your pleasures during your life, when Lazarus suffered; now he has his consolation and you are in torments. What is more, a great gulf has been placed between you and us, so that no one who might wish to cross from here to you and back again can do so." He replied: "Then, father, I ask you to send him to my father's house, where I have five brothers to bring them a warning, or else they too may come to this place of torment." But Abraham said: "They have Moses and the prophets; let them listen to them!" But he said: "Not they, father Abraham! But if someone comes back from the dead to visit them, they will repent." Abraham replied: "If they do not heed Moses and the prophets, they will not be convinced even if someone should rise from the dead."'

(Lk 16:19-31)

Faith works miracles. Humility of believers: we are worthless servants

The apostles said to the Lord: 'Give us greater faith'; and the Lord replied: 'If your faith were even as big as a mustard seed, you could command this mulberry tree to take up its roots and plant them in the sea, and it would obey you.

'If you have a slave working for you at the plough or with the sheep, do you say to him, when he comes back from the fields, "Come straight to the table"? Do you not rather say, "Get my supper ready; bestir yourself, and wait on me while I eat and drink; you can have your own supper afterwards"? Are you indebted to the slave for doing what he was ordered to do? So too with you: when you have done all that you have been given to do, you must say: "We are but worthless servants; we have done no more than our duty."'

(Lk 17:5-10)

The ten lepers: only one is saved, that is, cured in soul as well as body

While Jesus was on his journey to Jerusalem, he passed between Samaria and Galilee. He was entering one of the villages, when he was met by ten lepers, who stood at a distance and raised their voices, crying: 'Jesus, Master, have pity on us.' Jesus saw them and said: 'Go and show yourselves to the priests.' They went; and on the way they were made clean. One of them, when he saw that he had been cured, came back praising God in a loud voice, and fell prostrate at Jesus' feet, and thanked him. Now this man was a Samaritan. So Jesus said: 'Were not all ten made clean? Where are the other nine? Has none of them returned to give glory to God, but only this foreigner?' Then he said to the man: 'Rise up and go; your faith has saved you.'

(Lk 17:11-19)

The mystery of the kingdom of God: already present but not yet realised

Once, when he was asked by the Pharisees to say when the kingdom of God would come, he replied: 'There are no portents to observe when the kingdom of God comes. There will be no day when people can say, "Look, here it is!" or "There it is!" No, the kingdom of God is already among you.'

He said to the disciples: 'The time will come when you will long to see one of the Days of the Son of Man, and you will not see it.

'They will say to you, "Look, he is here!" and "Look, he is there!" But do not go off in search of him. For the appearance of the Son of Man, when his Day comes, will be like the brilliance of lightning, flashing across the sky from end to end. But first he must be rejected by this generation and suffer much.

'What happened in the days of Noah will happen again in the Days of the Son of Man. There was eating and drinking, marrying and giving in marriage, up to the day when Noah went into the Ark, and the flood came and destroyed them all.

'The same happened in the days of Lot: men were eating and drinking, buying and selling, planting and building; but on the day when Lot came out of Sodom, fire and brimstone poured down from heaven and destroyed them all. It will be the same on the Day when the Son of Man is revealed.

'On that day, if a man is on the roof and his goods are in the house, when he comes down he must not fetch them out, and the man who is in the fields must not turn back. Remember Lot's wife! Whoever strives to preserve his life will lose it, and whoever loses it will save it.'

(Lk 17:20-33)

The unjust judge: God approves of persistent prayer

He also told them a parable to show that they must pray at all times and not lose heart. 'There was once a judge,' he said, 'in a certain town, who had no fear of God and no regard for man. And in the same town lived a widow who kept coming to him and saying, "Give me redress against my enemy." For a long time he refused, but at length he said to himself, "It is not that I fear God or have any regard for man, but this widow is a nuisance to me, so I shall give her redress, and then she will not be for ever coming to plague me."' Then the Lord said: 'Mark those words of the unjust judge, and tell me, will not God vindicate his own chosen ones who cry to him night and day? Will he be slow to aid them? I tell you, he will vindicate them without delay. Even so, when the Son of Man comes will he find faith upon the earth?'

(Lk 18:1-8)

The Pharisee and the tax-gatherer: prayer is born of humility

He also spoke a parable against certain persons who were confident of their own justice and looked down on the rest of men: 'Two men went up into the temple to pray; one was a Pharisee, the other a tax-gatherer. The Pharisee stood there and prayed to himself like this: "O God, I thank you that I am not like the rest of men, greedy, unjust, adulterer — like this tax-gatherer here. I fast twice a week, and I pay tithes on my whole income." But the tax-gatherer stood at a distance and would not so much as raise his eyes to heaven, but kept beating his breast and repeating, "O God, be merciful to me, sinner that I am!" I tell you he, rather than the other, went home justified. For everyone who exalts himself will be humbled, and he who humbles himself will be exalted.'

(Lk 18:9-14)

The rich young man: keeping the commandments is useless without being at God's disposal

As he was setting out on a journey, a man ran up and knelt before him: 'Good master,' he said, 'what must I do to gain everlasting life?' Jesus said to him: 'Why do you call me "good"? God alone is good and no one else! You know the commandments: *do not kill, do not commit adultery, do not steal, do not bear false witness*, commit no fraud, *honour your father and your mother.*' But he answered: 'Master, I have kept all those commandments since I was young.' Jesus looked at him with love and said: 'There remains one thing that you have not done: go and sell all you have, and give the money to the poor, and you will have treasure in heaven; then come back and follow me, and bear your cross.' At these words his face fell and he turned sadly away, for he owned great wealth.

Jesus looked round at his disciples and said: 'How hard it is for the wealthy to gain entry into the kingdom of God!' The disciples were amazed at this; but Jesus only repeated what he had said: 'Children, how hard it is for those who place their trust in wealth to enter the kingdom of God! It is easier for a camel to pass through the eye of a needle, than for a rich man to enter the kingdom of God.' They were even more amazed, and said to him: 'If that is so, who can be saved?' Jesus looked at them and said: 'With men it is impossible, but not with God. All things are possible with God.'

Peter said to him: 'What of us! We have left everything and followed you!' Jesus answered: 'I tell you truly, everyone who has left home or brothers or sisters or mother or father or children or lands for my sake and for the sake of the gospel, will receive a hundred-fold now in this world: houses, brothers, sisters, mothers, children, land — but also persecutions — and he will receive everlasting life in the world to come. And many who are now first will be last, and the last will be first.'

(Mk 10:17-31)

The labourers in the vineyard: God calls at any time, first Israel, then the Gentiles

'For the kingdom of heaven is like this. A householder went out early in the morning to hire labourers for his vineyard. He made an agreement with the labourers that he would pay them a silver piece for the day's work, and sent them off into his vineyard. About nine o'clock, he went out again, and seeing some more men standing about idle in the market place, he said to them: "You too, go into my vineyard, and I shall pay you a fair wage." So off they went. Again about midday and at three in the afternoon, he went out and did the same. At last, about five o'clock he went out and found still more men standing there; and he said to them: "Why do you stand here idle all the day?" They replied: "No one has hired us." So he said to them: "You too, go into the vineyard." When evening came, the owner of the vineyard said to his steward: "Call the labourers and pay them their wages, beginning with the last and ending with the first." Those hired at five o'clock came and received a silver piece. So when the first came, they expected to be paid more; but they too received the silver piece. At this they began to grumble against the owner: "These last," they said, "have done only one hour's work, and you have treated them the same as us, who have been toiling all day in the heat." In reply, the owner said to one of them: "My good friend, I do you no wrong. You settled with me for a silver piece, did you not? Then take your pay and be off. I mean to give the same to this last man as to you. Am I not allowed to do as I wish with what is my own? Or are you scowling at me because I am generous?" That is how it will be: the first will be last and the last will be first.'
(Mt 20:1-16)

Jesus welcomes and blesses children who have privileges in his kingdom

People began to bring little children for him to touch, but the disciples scolded them. Jesus was indignant when he saw this and said to them: 'Let the little children come to me; do not stop them; the kingdom of God belongs to such as these. I tell you truly, anyone who does not receive the kingdom of God like a little child will not enter it at all.' Then he embraced the children, and laid his hands on them, and blessed them.
(Mk 10:13-16)

Jesus goes to Bethany because his friend Lazarus is sick

A man named Lazarus lay ill at the village of Bethany, where Mary and her sister Martha lived. (This Mary is the woman who anointed the Lord with ointment and wiped his feet with her hair, and Lazarus who was ill was her brother.) The sisters sent this message to Jesus: 'Lord, one whom you love is ill.' When Jesus heard it, he said: 'This illness is not to end in death; it is for the glory of God; through this illness the glory of the Son of God will be revealed.' That is why, although Jesus loved Martha and her sister and Lazarus, for two days after hearing of his illness he stayed where he was. Then he said to his disciples: 'Let us go back into Judea.' 'Rabbi,' they replied, 'will you go back? Why, only just now the Jews attempted to stone you!' Jesus answered: 'Is it not true that there are twelve hours in the day, and if a man walks by daylight, he does not stumble, because he sees the light of this world; whereas if he walks by night, he does stumble, because he has no light?' Then he added: 'Our friend Lazarus has fallen asleep; I shall go and wake him.' The disciples replied: 'Lord, if he has fallen asleep, he will recover.' For they thought that Jesus had spoken of ordinary sleep, whereas he meant the sleep of death. So he said to them in plain words: 'Lazarus is dead; and I am glad I was not there — glad for your sakes, for the strengthening of your faith. But come, let us go to him.' Then Thomas, called "the Twin", said to his fellow disciples: 'Come, let us go too, and die with him!'

(Jn 11:1-16)

Jesus, the good shepherd, restores Lazarus to life

When Jesus arrived, he found that Lazarus had already been four days in the tomb. As Bethany was not far from Jerusalem — less than two miles in fact — many of the Jews had come out to Martha and Mary, to console them over the loss of their brother. When Martha was told that Jesus was coming, she went out to meet him while Mary remained sitting at home. Martha said to Jesus: 'Lord, if you had been here, my brother would not have died; and even now I know that whatever you ask of God, he will grant you.' Jesus said to her: 'I am resurrection and I am life. Whoever believes in me, even though he dies, will yet live; he who lives and believes in me will never die. Do you believe this?' 'Yes, Lord,' she replied, 'I do believe it, because you are the Messiah, the Son of God, the one who was to come into the world.' After saying this, she went away and called her sister Mary aside privately and said to her: 'The Master is here and is asking for you.'

When Mary heard this, she rose up quickly and went to Jesus. (He had not yet entered the village, but was still in the place where Martha had met him.) When the Jews who were there to console her saw her suddenly rise up and leave the house, they followed her, for they thought she was going to weep at the tomb. Mary reached the place where Jesus was, and as soon as she saw him she fell at his feet and cried out: 'Lord, if only you had been here, my brother would not have died.' When Jesus saw that she was weeping and that the Jews who had come with her were weeping too, he was himself deeply moved and sorely upset. 'Where have you laid him?' he said. They replied: 'Lord, come and see,' and Jesus was moved to tears. The Jews said: 'See how much he loved him!' But some of them said: 'If he opened the blind man's eyes, could he not have saved Lazarus from dying?'

Jesus was again deeply moved when he arrived at the tomb. It was a cave with a stone sealing it, and Jesus gave word to remove the stone. Martha, the dead man's sister, said: 'But Lord, by now there will be a bad smell; he has been here four days.' Jesus replied: 'Did I not tell you that if you believe, you will see the glory of God?' So they removed the stone. Jesus then lifted his eyes upwards and said: "Father, I give you thanks because you have heard my prayer. I know that you hear me always, but I have spoken aloud for the sake of the people who stand round me, so that they will believe that you have sent me.' After this prayer, he called out in a loud voice: 'Lazarus, come out!' The dead man came out with his hands and feet wrapped in bands of linen and his face covered with a cloth. Jesus said to the bystanders: 'Untie him and let him go free.'

(Jn 11:17-44)

The leaders of Israel decide on the death of Jesus

When Mary's Jewish visitors saw what Jesus had done, many of them believed in him; but some of them went away and reported it all to the Pharisees. So the chief priests and Pharisees called a meeting of the Sanhedrin and said: 'What are we doing? This man is performing many miracles. If we let him go on like this, everyone will believe in him, and the Romans will come and destroy both our holy place and our nation.' But one of them, Caiaphas, who was High Priest that year, said to them: 'Are you so ignorant? Do you not see that it is necessary for you that one man should die for the people, and not the whole nation perish?' He did not say this of himself, but being High Priest that year, he spoke as a prophet, announcing that Jesus would die for the Jewish nation — and not for the Jewish nation alone, but also to gather and unite the scattered children of God.

From that day they were determined to put Jesus to death. So he could no longer go about openly among the Jews, but withdrew to a city called Ephraim on the borders of the desert, and stayed there with his disciples.

(Jn 11:45-54)

Jesus called out
in a loud voice:
'Lazarus,
come out!'
The dead man
came out with
his hands and feet
wrapped in bands
of linen

Jesus foretells the cup of martyrdom, while Zebedee's sons are ambitious for high places

They were on the road, going up to Jerusalem, and Jesus was walking ahead of them. They were in deep distress, and those following behind were afraid. Then he again took the Twelve to his side, and told them what was about to happen to him: 'We are now going up to Jerusalem,' he said, 'and the Son of Man will be betrayed to the chief priests and the scribes, who will condemn him to death and hand him over to the Gentiles; he will be mocked and spat upon, and scourged and put to death; and after three days he will rise again.'

James and John, the sons of Zebedee, came up and said to him: 'Master, will you grant us one request, what ever it may be?' He replied: 'What do you want me to do for you?' They said: 'Let us sit one at your right and one at your left, when you are in glory.' Jesus said to them: 'You do not know what you are asking. Can you drink the chalice that I am to dring, or undergo the baptism that I am to undergo?' They answered: 'We can.' Jesus said to them: 'You will indeed drink of the chalice that I am to drink, and undergo the baptism that I am to undergo; but to sit on my right or on my left is not mine to give; it belongs to those for whom it is reserved.'

When the other ten heard about this request, they were indignant with James and John. So Jesus called them all to him and said to them: 'You know that the mighty rulers of the Gentiles lord it over their subjects, and their great men reign like tyrants. This cannot be so among you. Whoever wants to become a great man among you must become your servant; and whoever wants to be the first among you must become the slave of you all. For the Son of Man himself has not come to be served but to serve, and to offer his life as a ransom for many.' (Mk 10:32-45)

The blind man of Jericho is cured by his faith

So they came to Jericho. A blind beggar called Bartimaeus, son of Timaeus, was sitting by the roadside, when Jesus left the city with his disciples and a large crowd accompanying him. When he heard that it was Jesus of Nazareth, he cried out: 'Son of David, Jesus, have pity on me!' Many of the people told him sharply to keep quiet, but he cried out still louder: 'Son of David, have pity on me!' Jesus stopped and said: 'Call him over.' They called the blind man: 'Courage!' they said, 'Stand up! He is calling you.' He threw off his cloak, leaped up, and came to Jesus. Jesus said to him: 'What do you want me to do for you?' The blind man said: 'Rabboni, let me have back my sight!' Jesus said to him: 'Go, your faith has saved you.' At once he recovered his sight; and he followed Jesus along the road. (Mk 10:46-52)

Talk with Zacchaeus, chief of the tax-gatherers

So he entered Jericho and was going through its streets. A certain Zacchaeus, one of the chief tax-gatherers and a rich man, wanted to know what Jesus looked like, but could not see him for the crowd, as he was not tall enough. So he hastened ahead and climbed a sycamore tree to see him, because he knew he would pass that way. When Jesus came to the place, he looked up and said to him: 'Zacchaeus, come down quickly! I must stay at your house tonight.' So he came down at once, and gladly made him welcome. But those who observed this all grumbled because he had gone to lodge with a sinner. Zacchaeus, however, stood there and said to the Lord: 'I wish to say this, Lord: I am going to give half my property to the poor, and if I have defrauded anyone, I will repay him four times over.' Jesus said to him: 'Today salvation has come to this house, for this man too has proved himself a son of Abraham. The Son of Man has come to seek and save what was lost.'

(Lk 19:1-10)

Parable of the talents: God's gifts must not be kept under ground

While they were listening to him, he told them another parable, because he was now close to Jerusalem and they imagined that the kingdom of God was about to appear forthwith. 'A man of high birth,' he said, 'made a journey to a distant country, to obtain for himself the title of king and then come back. But first he summoned ten of his servants and gave them each ten pounds and said: "Use this for trading until I come back." His subjects hated him and sent an embassy, close on his heels, to say: "We do not want this man to be our king." Nevertheless he did obtain the kingship. When he came back, he summoned the servants to whom he had given the money, to hear the result of each man's trading. The first came and said: "Sir, your ten pounds have earned a hundred more." He said to him: "Well done, my good servant! You have proved trustworthy in this very small matter; you will have authority over ten cities." The second came and said: "Your ten pounds, sir, have made fifty more." The king said to him: "You will have five cities under your control." But another came and said: "Sir, here are your ten pounds — I kept them wrapped up in a napkin. I was afraid of you, because you are a severe man. You take profits without taking risks, and reap what you have not sown." The king replied: "Wretched servant! By your own words I condemn you. You knew that I am a severe man, taking profits without taking risks and reaping without having sown. Why then did you not put my money into a bank? Then I could have come and drawn it out with interest." And he told his attendants to take the ten pounds away from him and give them to the one with the hundred pounds. "But sir," they said, "he has a hundred pounds already." "I tell you," he replied, "to everyone who has plenty more will be given; but from him who has little, even what he has will be taken away."'

(Lk 19:11-26)

he Jewish Passover was at hand, and many people went up to Jerusalem from the country to purify themselves before the Passover. They looked for Jesus and said to one another, as they stood about in the temple: 'What do you think? He will not come to the feast, will he?' For the chief priests and Pharisees had given orders that anyone who knew his whereabouts was to inform them, so that they could arrest him.

(Jn 11:55-57)

**Prophetic anointing
of Jesus as king
and priest**

Six days before the Passover, Jesus came to Bethany, the home of Lazarus, whom he had raised from the dead. A supper was given in his honour, at which Martha waited on them, and Lazarus was among those at table with him. Mary brought a pound of costly spikenard ointment and anointed the feet of Jesus and wiped them with her hair, and the house was filled with the fragrance of the ointment. But one of his disciples, Judas Iscariot, the one who was later to betray him, said: 'Why was not this ointment sold for three hundred silver pieces, and the money given to the poor?' He said this, not because he had any concern for the poor, but because he was a thief; he kept the common purse and used to steal what was put into it. But Jesus said: 'Leave her alone! Let her keep the rest for the day of my burial. The poor you have with you always, but you will not always have me.'

Many of the Jews heard that Jesus was at Bethany and came out, not only because of him, but also to see Lazarus whom he had raised from the dead. So the chief priests decided to kill Lazarus too, because many of the Jews were going off and believing in Jesus on account of him.

(Jn 12:1-11)

PALM SUNDAY

Triumphal entry of Jesus, King and Messiah, in Jerusalem

When approaching Bethphage and Bethany on the Mount of Olives, Jesus sent ahead two of the disciples: 'Go into the village over there,' he said, 'and as you go in, you will find tethered there a colt which no one has yet mounted. Untie it and bring it here. If anyone asks you why you are untying it, say, "The master has need of it."' The messengers went off and found everything as he had said, as they were untying the colt, the owners did ask: "Why are you untying that colt?" and they replied: "The Master has need of it." So they brought it to Jesus, and put their cloaks over its back, for Jesus to mount. As he rode along, people spread their cloaks in the road. When he arrived at the descent from the Mount of Olives, the whole throng of his disciples began to praise God with joy for all the miracles they had seen; they cried aloud: '*Blessed be he that is coming* as king *in the name of the Lord!* Peace in heaven, and glory on high!'

Some Pharisees who were among the crowd said to him: 'Master, restrain your disciples!' But he replied: 'I tell you, if they remain silent, the very stones will cry out.'   (Lk 19:29-40)

Jesus weeps over the blind obstinacy of the holy city

When he came closer still and the city came in sight, he wept over it and said: 'If you had but known today the things that make for peace! As it is, they are hidden from your eyes. The days will come when your enemies will erect a rampart against you, besiege you and hem you in on every side. They will dash you to the ground, and your children within you, and will not leave one stone upon another, because you did not recognise your opportunity when the Lord visited you.'

The disciples did not understand this at the time, but after Jesus had been glorified, they remembered that these things had been done for him, and saw that the Scriptures had spoken of him. The people who had been with him when he had called Lazarus from the tomb and raised him from the dead never ceased bearing witness to him. That was why the people came to meet him in such numbers: they had heard that he had performed this miracle. But the Pharisees were saying to one another: 'It is clear that we are making no progress. Look! The whole world has gone after him!'   (Lk 19:41-44; Jn 12:16-19)

128

Jesus shows the meaning of his death to the Gentiles also

Among the pilgrims who had come up to worship at the feast were some Greeks. They approached Philip, who was from Bethsaida in Galilee, and said: 'Sir, we should like to see Jesus.' Philip went and spoke to Andrew; then Andrew and Philip went and told Jesus.

In answer, Jesus said to them: 'The hour has come! The Son of Man is now to be glorified. I tell you truly, if a grain of wheat does not fall to the earth and die, it remains a single grain; but if it dies, it yields a plentiful harvest. The man who loves his life ruins it, and the man who hates his life in this world preserves it for eternal life. If anyone wishes to serve me, let him follow me; and where I am, there too my servant will be. The Father will honour him who serves me.

'Now my soul is in turmoil; and what shall I say? "Father, save me from this hour?" But it is for this that I have come: for this very hour! Father, glorify your name!' Then a voice came from heaven: 'I have glorified it and shall glorify it again.' Some of the people who stood listening thought it had thundered; others said: 'An angel has spoken to him.' But Jesus said to them: 'The voice did not speak for my sake, but for yours.

'Now is the judgement of this world; now the ruler of this world is to be driven out; and I myself, when I am lifted up off the earth, shall draw all men to myself.' This he said to signify the manner of death by which he was about to die.

The people answered: 'We have heard from the law that the Messiah is to remain for ever; how then can you say that the Son of Man must be lifted up? Who is this Son of Man?' Jesus said to them: 'Still for a while the Light is among you. Walk while you have the Light, or the darkness will overtake you. The man who walks in the darkness does not know where he is going. While you have the Light, believe in the Light, and so become sons of Light.' (Jn 12:20-36)

MONDAY IN HOLY WEEK

Cursing of the barren fig tree

Jesus entered Jerusalem and went into the temple; and after looking all round, since it was now late, he went out to Bethany with the Twelve.

The next day, when they set out from Bethany, Jesus was hungry. He saw a fig-tree in leaf some distance away, and went to see if he could find anything on it. But when he came to it, he found nothing but leaves; for figs were not yet in season. Then he said to the tree, in the hearing of his disciples: 'May no one ever eat fruit from you again!' (Mk 11:11-14)

**The decisive meeting
of Jesus and the
enemies who are
unwilling to believe**

In the morning, as they passed by, they saw that the fig-tree had withered root and branch. Peter remembered and said to Jesus: 'Rabbi, look! The fig-tree which you cursed has withered! Jesus replied: 'Have faith in God. I tell you truly, if anyone says to this mountain: "Rise up and throw yourself into the sea," and does not doubt in his heart, but believes that what he says will be done for him, then it will be so!

'Therefore I say to you, whatever you ask for in prayer, believe that you have received it, and you will have it!

'Whenever you stand praying, if you have any grievance against anyone, forgive him. Then your Father who is in heaven will also forgive you your transgressions.'

Then he went into the temple, and the chief priests and elders of the people came to him while he was teaching, and said: 'Explain your powers, by which you do these things: who gave you these powers?' Jesus replied: 'I too have a question for you; if you give me the answer, I will then explain the powers by which I do these things. The baptism administered by John — was that from heaven, or was it of human origin?' They reasoned among themselves: 'If we say it was from heaven, he will retort, "Then why did you not believe him?" But we can hardly say it was of human origin — for fear of the people, because they all regard John as a prophet.' So they said to Jesus: 'We do not know.' And he in turn said to them: 'Then I do not explain to you the powers by which I do these things.'

(Mk 11:20-25; Mt 21: 23-27)

**Parable of the two
sons: it is better to
believe actively than
merely formally**

'But what do you think about this? A man had two sons. He went to the first and said: "Son, go and work in the vineyard today." He replied: "Certainly, sir!" but he did not go. Then the man went to his second son and gave the same order. He replied: "I don't want to," but afterward he regretted it and went. Which of the two did his father's will?' They answered: 'The second'. Jesus said to them: 'I tell you truly, tax-gatherers and harlots are showing you the way into the kingdom of God. For John came to show you the way of justice, and you did not believe him; but tax-gatherers and harlots did believe him. You saw them, and yet even then you did not change your minds and believe him.'

(Mt 21:28-32)

**The wicked vine-
dressers: the kingdom
will be given to the
Gentiles**

'Listen to another parable: A landowner once planted a vineyard, and put a fence round it, and dug a winepress and built a tower in it; then he let it out to tenants and went abroad. When vintage-time was near, he sent his servants to the tenants to collect his produce.

But the tenants took hold of his servants, beat one, killed another, and stoned a third. Then he sent other servants, a larger number than before, and these were treated in the same way. Later he sent his son to them, for he thought they would respect his son. But when the tenants saw the son, they said to one another: "This is the heir. Come on, let us kill him and take his inheritance." So they seized him, threw him out of the vineyard, and killed him. Tell me then: when the owner of the vineyard comes, what will he do to those tenants?' They answered: 'He will bring those bad men to a bad end, and let out the vineyard to other tenants, who will give him the products when it is due.'

Jesus said to them: 'Have you never read in the Scriptures: *The stone which the builders rejected has been made the corner stone; this is the Lord's doing, and is wonderful in our eyes?* So I tell you, the kingdom of God will be taken away from you, and given to a people that does yield its produce. The man who falls upon this stone will be crushed.'

The chief priests and Pharisees listening to his parables knew that it was about themselves that he was speaking. They wanted to arrest him; but they were afraid of the people, who regarded him as a prophet.

(Mt 21:33-46)

The tribute-money: Caesar's rule is important, but God comes first

Then the Pharisees went away and plotted how to trap him in an argument. They sent their own disciples to him and with them some of Herod's courtiers. 'Master,' they said, 'we know that you speak the truth and truly teach the way of God; you are afraid of no one, and are not swayed by human respect. Tell us therefore, what is your view? Is it lawful to pay taxes to Caesar or not?' Jesus saw through their malice, and said: 'Why do you try to trap me, you hypocrites? Show me a coin in which the tax is paid.' They produced a silver coin, and he said to them: 'Whose is the image and inscription?' 'Caesar's,' they replied. He said to them: 'Then render to Caesar the things that are Caesar's and to God the things that are God's.' This answer came as a surprise to them; so they left him alone and went away.

(Mt 22:15-22)

God will make the dead arise, for he is God of living people

On that day, some of the Sadducees came to him, maintaining that there is no resurrection. The question they put to him was this: 'Master, Moses said: *If a man dies childless, his brother must marry the widow and beget children in his brother's name.* We had a case of seven brothers: the first married and died; having no children, he left the widow to his brother. The same happened with the second, and the third, and so on to the seventh. After them all the woman died. Now at the resurrection, to which of the seven will the woman belong? For she has been the wife of each of them!' Jesus answered them: 'You are in error, and the reason is that you do not understand the Scriptures or the power of God. Once risen, men and women do not marry; they are as angels in heaven. As for proof of the resurrection of the dead, have you not read the words which God himself spoke to you: *I am the God of Abraham and the God of Isaac and the God of Jacob?* He is God not of dead men but of the living.' The people who heard him were filled with wonder at his teaching.

(Mt 22:23-33)

The first commandment is love for God and for one's neighbour

Then one of the scribes came forward. He had been listening to the dispute and recognised that Jesus had answered well. So he asked him: 'Which is the first commandment of all?' Jesus answered:

'The first is:
Hear, O Israel! The Lord our God is one Lord; and you shall love the Lord your God with your whole heart, and with your whole soul, and with your whole mind, and with your whole strength.
The second is:
You shall love your neighbour as your self.
There is no other commandment greater than these.'

The scribe said to him: 'Admirable, Master! You have spoken truly, for God is one and there is no other but He, and to love him with your whole heart, and with your whole understanding, and with your whole strength, and to love your neighbour as yourself, is something far greater than all holocausts and sacrifices.' Jesus acknowledged that he had spoken wisely by saying to him: 'You are not far from the kingdom of God.'

(Mk 12:28-34)

The only true
teacher is Christ:
the others are so
in name only

Then Jesus spoke to the people and to his disciples. 'Since the scribes and the Pharisees,' he said, 'have occupied the chair of Moses you must heed and do all that they say to you. But do not imitate what they do, for they do not obey their own teaching. They bind heavy and unbearable burdens and pile them on other men's shoulders, but themselves never stir a finger to move them.

'All that they do is done to be seen by men: they widen their phylacteries and broaden the hems of their cloaks; they love to have places of honour at banquets and the first seats in the synagogues, to be bowed to in the market-places and addressed by the people as "Rabbi". But you must not take the title of "Rabbi"; there is one master over you, and you are all brothers. And do not address anyone on earth as your "Father"; there is only one father for you, your Father in heaven. And do not take the title of "Teacher"; you must have only one Teacher, Christ.

'The greatest among you must be your servant; whoever exalts himself will be humbled; and whoever humbles himself will be exalted.'

(Mt 23:1-12)

Indictment of
the hypocrisy of
the scribes and
Pharisees

'But woe to you, scribes and Pharisees! Hypocrites! You shut the gates of the kingdom of heaven in men's faces. You neither go in yourselves, nor allow others to enter.

'Woe to you, scribes and Pharisees! Hypocrites! You journey by land and sea to make a single proselyte, and when it is done, you make him twice as fit for hell as you are yourselves.

'Woe to you, blind guides that you are! You say that if a man swears by the temple, the oath is invalid; but if he swears by the gold of the temple, he is bound by his oath. You are fools and blind! Which is greater, the gold, or the temple that sanctifies the gold? And again you say, that if a man swears by the altar, the oath is invalid; but if he swears by the offering placed on the altar, he is bound by his oath. You are blind! Which is greater, the offering, or the altar that sanctifies the gift? Very well then! A man who swears by the altar swears both by the altar and by everything on it; a man who swears by the temple swears both by the temple and by him who dwells in it; and a man who swears by heaven swears both by God's throne and by him who sits enthroned.

'Woe to you, scribes and Pharisees! Hypocrites! You pay tithes on mint, anise and cummin; but you have neglected the weightier things which the Law demands — justice, mercy, fidelity. These are the commandments you should have observed, without neglecting those others. You are blind guides! Straining off gnats and swallowing camels!

'Woe to you, scribes and Pharisees! Hypocrites! You clean the outside of cup and plate, when inside there is a lining of rapacity and extortion. Blind Pharisee! First clean the inside of the cup; after that the outside too can be cleaned.

'Woe to you, scribes and Pharisees! Hypocrites! You are like whited sepulchres that look well outside but inside are full of dead men's bones and every kind of corruption. So too with you: outside you look like just men, but inside you are full of hypocrisy and wickedness.

'Woe to you, scribes and Pharisees! Hypocrites! You build fine sepulchres and monuments for prophets and just men, and you say "If we had lived in the days of our forefathers, we should have had no part in shedding the blood of the prophets." If then you confess yourselves the sons of those who murdered the prophets, bring to full measure the work that your fathers began!

'Snakes! Sons of vipers! How are you going to escape damnation in hell? I am sending to you prophets and sages and scribes: some you will kill and crucify, others you will scourge in your synagogues, and hunt from city to city. And why? To bring upon you all the innocent blood spilt on the earth, from the blood of innocent Abel to the blood of Zechariah, son of Barachiah, whom you butchered between the sanctuary and the altar. I tell you truly, all this will fall upon the present generation.'

(Mt 23:13-36)

In the sight of God it is generosity which matters, not wealth

Once he sat down facing the treasury and was watching the people as they dropped money into the coffers. Many rich people were dropping in large sums. Then a poor widow came and dropped in two tiny coins worth halfpenny. Jesus called his disciples to him and said to them: 'I tell you truly, of all the people making offerings to the treasury this poor widow has given the most; for what they gave of their ample means still left them with plenty, but she has given all her meagre store, the whole of her livelihood.'

(Mk 12:41-44)

PROPHETIC VISION OF THE LAST DAYS

The end of Jerusalem is an image and prophecy of the end of the world

Then Jesus went out of the temple. As he was leaving, his disciples came and drew his attention to the fine buildings of the temple. But he said to them: 'You see all this? I tell you truly, not one stone of it will be left on another; all will be thrown down.'

He went to the Mount of Olives and sat down; and his disciples came to him privately and said: 'Tell us, when will this happen? And what sign will there be of your Coming, and of the end of this present age?'

Jesus answered them: 'Take care that no one leads you astray. For many a man will come using my name and saying, "I am the Messiah," and many will be misled. You will hear of wars and rumours of wars. But do not be alarmed; these things must happen, but still it will not be the end. For nation will rise against nation, and kingdom against kingdom, and there will be plagues, famines and earthquakes in many places. All this is but the beginning of the birth-pangs.

'Then you will be given up to torture and death; and you will be hated by all nations because of my name. Many will fall away; they will betray one another and hate one another. Many false prophets will appear, and will lead many astray. And as lawlessness abounds, so charity will grow cold throughout the world. But the man who remains steadfast to the end will be saved. This gospel of the kingdom must be proclaimed throughout the world to make it known to all the nations. Then the end will come.

'When, therefore, you see *the abomination of desolation*, of which the prophet Daniel spoke, *standing in a holy place* (let the reader mark this well!), those who are in Judea must take to the mountains; the man who is on the housetop, when he comes down, must not fetch anything from his house, and the man who is in the fields must not turn back to fetch his coat. It will go hard with women who are with child or have babes at the breast in those days! Pray that your flight may not be in winter or on the sabbath, for it will be a *day of misery* greater then *has ever been since the beginning of the world*, or ever will be again. Indeed if the time of destruction had not been shortened, not one human being would survive; but for the sake of the elect it will be cut short.'

(Mt 24:1-22)

The Messiah will return to bring justice to the oppressed

'If anyone then says to you, "Look, here is the Messiah!" or "He is there," do not believe it. False messiahs and false prophets will appear and work great signs and wonders, to mislead, if it were possible, even the elect. Mark this well, I have forewarned you.

'If, then, you are told, "He is out in the desert," do not go out; if you are told, "He is lurking in hiding," do not believe it. For the Coming of the Son of Man will be as clearly seen as lightning flashing across from the east to the west. Wherever the corpse is, there the vultures will gather.

'Immediately after the distress of those days,

*the sun will be darkened,
and the moon will not give her light;
stars will fall from the heavens,
and the powers on high will be rocked.*

'Then the sign of the Son of Man will be seen in the heavens; and *all the peoples of the earth will beat their breasts, as they behold the Son of Man coming upon the clouds of heaven* with great power and glory. With a great trumpet-blast he will send out his angels, who will gather in his elect from the four winds, from the furthest regions under heaven.'

(Mt 24:23-31)

The end of Jerusalem is near: Jesus' return, however, will come as unexpectedly as a thief

'Let the fig-tree teach you a lesson. As soon as its branches grow tender and break into leaf, you know that summer is near. In the same way, when you see all this, know that he is at hand, at your very door.

'I tell you truly, this generation will not have passed away before all these things happen. Heaven and earth will pass away, but my words will remain. No one knows the day or the hour when all this will happen, not even the angels in heaven, but only the Father.

'At the coming of the Son of Man there will be a repetition of what happened in the time of Noah. In the days before the flood there was eating and drinking, marrying and giving in marriage, up to the day when Noah went into the ark, and men were quite unconcerned until the flood came and swept them all away. The same will happen at the coming of the Son of Man. Two men will be working in a field, one will be taken, and one will be left; two women will be grinding at the handmill, one will be taken, and one will be left. Watch, therefore, for you do not know on what day your Lord is coming.'

(Mt 24:32-42)

The waiting must be joyful: the Lord's coming will be like a wedding-feast

'The kingdom of heaven will be like this. Ten bridesmaids once took their lamps and went out to meet the bridegroom. Five of them were foolish and five were prudent. The foolish ones took only their lamps with them, but no supply of oil; but the prudent ones took flasks of oil as well as their lamps. As the bridegroom was a long time coming, they all dozed off to sleep. But at midnight there was a cry: "Here is the bridegroom, come out and meet him!" At this, all the bridesmaids bestirred themselves and trimmed their lamps; and the foolish ones said to the prudent ones: "Give us some of your oil, because our lamps are going out." But the prudent ones replied: "We doubt if we have enough for you as well; you had better go to the oil sellers and buy some." While they were on their way to the shop, the bridegroom came; those who were ready went in with him to the wedding-banquet, and the door was shut. Later the other bridesmaids came back, and called: "Lord, Lord, open the door for us." But he replied: "I tell you truly, I do not know you." Be on the watch then, for you do not know the day or the hour.'

(Mt 25:1-13)

140

'When the Son of Man comes in his glory and all the angels with him he will sit on his throne of glory, and all the nations will be assembled before him. Then he will separate them out, as a shepherd parts the sheep from the goats, he will make the sheep stand at his right, and the goats at his left. Then the King will say to those at his right: "You whom my Father has blessed: come, take possession of the kingdom that has been prepared for you from the foundation of the world. For

> I was hungry and you gave me food;
> I was thirsty and you gave me clothes;
> I was ill and you looked after me;
> I was in prison and you visited me."

Then the just will reply:

> "Lord, when did we see you hungry
> and give you food,
> or thirsty and give you drink?
> When did we see you a foreigner and make you welcome,
> or when did we see you naked and give you clothes?
> When did we see you ill or in prison
> and visit you?"

Then the King will reply: "I tell you truly, whatever you did for one of the lowliest of these my brothers, you did for me."

'Then he will speak to those on his left: 'You who are accursed: depart from me into the everlasting fire prepared for the devil and his angels. For

> I was hungry and you did not give me food;
> I was thirsty and you did not give me drink;
> I was a foreigner and you did not make me welcome;
> I was naked, and you did not give me clothes;
> I was ill, and in prison, and you did not visit me."

Then they too will reply:

"Lord, when was it that we saw you hungry or thirsty or a foreigner or without clothing or ill or in prison, and did not help you?" And he will reply: "I tell you truly, whatever you omitted to do for one of the lowliest of these, you omitted to do for me." Then these will go away to everlasting punishment, but the just to everlasting life.' (Mt 25:31-46)

SPY WEDNESDAY

Judas' plot to betray Jesus

When Jesus had finished this discourse, he turned to his disciples and said: 'At the Passover, which, as you know, is now two days off, the Son of Man will be handed over to be crucified.'

Then the chief priests and elders of the people foregathered in the court of the High Priest, whose name was Caiaphas; and they plotted how to take Jesus unawares, seize him, and put him to death. 'But,' they said, 'it must not be done during the festival, or there may be a riot among the people.'

Then one of the Twelve, the one called Judas Iscariot, went to the chief priests and said: 'What will you pay me to put him in your hands?' *They weighed out* for him *thirty silver pieces;* and from that time he began watching for an opportunity to betray him.   (Mt 26:1-5; 14-16)

MAUNDY THURSDAY: THE LORD'S SUPPER

Jesus has the Passover supper prepared

The day of Unleavened Bread arrived, when the Paschal lamb had to be sacrificed. Jesus therefore sent Peter and John ahead. 'Go,' he said, 'and make preparations for us to eat the Passover.' They asked: 'Where would you like us to make the preparations?' He replied: 'As you go into the city, you will meet a man carrying a jar of water; follow him, and say to the owner of the house which he enters: "The Master says: Where is the guest-room for me to eat the Passover with my disciples?" He will show you a large furnished room upstairs. Make the preparations there.' They went off and found everything just as he had told them, and made preparations for the Passover.

When it was time, he took his place at table with his apostles; and said to them: 'I have longed to eat this Passover with you before I suffer; for I tell you, I shall not eat it again before its fulfilment in the kingdom of God.' He took a cup, and gave thanks, and said: 'Take this and share it among you; for I tell you, from now on I shall not drink the fruit of the vine until God's kingdom comes.'   (Lk 22:7-18)

Jesus washes the disciples' feet, moving them towards the new venture of humble service

Already, before the Passover, Jesus was fully aware that his hour had come, and that he must pass over from this world to the Father. He had loved his own whom he was leaving in the world, and he gave them a supreme proof of his love.

They were at supper, and the devil had already put it into the heart of Judas son of Simon, the Iscariot, to play the traitor. Jesus, although he knew that the Father had entrusted all things into his hands, and that he had come from God and was going to God, rose from his place, put aside his clothes, and fastened a towel about his waist. Then he filled a jug with water and made to wash his disciples' feet and wipe them with the towel

'If then I,
though Lord and
Master, have washed
your feet, you too must
wash one another's feet'

which he had about him. He came to Simon Peter. But Peter protested: 'Lord, are you going to wash my feet!' Jesus replied: 'You do not understand at present what I am doing, but afterwards you will.' Peter said to him: 'No! You shall not wash my feet! Never!' Jesus replied: 'If I do not wash you, you have no part with me.' Simon Peter said to him: 'Lord, then wash not only my feet, but my hands and head as well.' Jesus answered: 'One who has bathed needs no further washing; he is wholly clean. You too are clean, though not every one of you.' For he knew the one who was about to betray him; that is why he said: 'Not every one of you is clean.'

When he had washed their feet and put on his clothes, he returned to his place and said to them: 'Understand what I have done for you. You call me "Master" and "Lord", and rightly so, for that is what I am. If then I, though Lord and Master, have washed your feet, you too must wash one another's feet. I have set you an example, so that you will do as I have done for you. I tell you truly, a servant is not greater than his lord, nor is an apostle greater than the one who sent him. Once you understand this, you will be blessed if you act upon it.

'I am not speaking of you all; I know the men whom I have chosen; but the Scripture must be fulfilled which says: *One who eats my bread has raised his heel against me.* I am telling you now before it is fulfilled, so that when it happens you will believe that I am what I say.

'I tell you truly, he who receives one whom I send receives me; and he who receives me receives the one who sent me.' (Jn 13:1-20)

The Eucharist begins in the betrayal: Judas has sold Christ

While saying this, Jesus was distressed in spirit, 'I tell you truly ,' he declared, 'one of you is about to betray me.' The disciples looked at one another, wondering whom he meant. One of them, the disciple whom Jesus loved, was reclining close to his bosom. So Simon Peter made a sign to him and said: 'Ask him who it is he means.' Then the disciple, without moving from his place, leaned back on to the breast of Jesus and said to him: 'Lord, who is it?' Jesus answered: 'The one to whom I give the piece of bread that I am dipping.' When he had dipped it, he gave it to Judas son of Simon, the Iscariot, who took the morsel. Then Satan entered him. Jesus said to him: 'Get your business over quickly!' None of those reclining at the table knew why Jesus had given him this order. As Judas kept the common purse, some thought that Jesus meant: 'Buy what we need for the feast,' or 'Give something to the poor.'

Judas, then, took the piece of bread and at once went out; and it was night.

When he had gone out, Jesus said: 'Now the Son of Man is glorified, and God is glorified in him! If God is glorified in him, God will also glorify him in himself; and he will do so without delay. My little ones, I

146

am with you now only for a while; you will look for me, but I say to you what I said to the Jews, "Where I am going, you cannot come."

'I give you a new commandment: you are to love one another, and to love one another as I have loved you. This is the mark by which all men will know you for my disciples; that you show love for one another.'

(Jn 13:21-35)

The disciples' betrayal: they discuss grandeur

A dispute arose among them as to which of them was to have the highest rank. But Jesus said to them: 'The kings of the Gentiles lord it over their subjects, and those who have authority over them take the title of "Benefactor". It must not be so among you! The eldest among you must be as the youngest, and the master as the servant who waits on him? For who is the greater, the one who sits at table or the servant who waits on him? Surely the one who sits at table. Yet I am like a servant among you.

'You are the men who have stayed with me through my trials. Therefore I covenant to you the kingly power which my Father has covenanted to me: you shall eat and drink at my table in the kingdom of God and sit on thrones ruling the twelve tribes of Israel.' (Lk 22:24-30)

Peter's betrayal: he will deny Jesus out of fear

'Simon, Simon, Satan has been given leave to sift you all like wheat. But I have prayed for you, Simon, that your faith may not fail; and once you have repented, you must strengthen your brethren.' Peter said to him: 'Lord, I am ready to face prison and death with you.' Jesus replied: 'I tell you, Peter, the cock will not crow tomorrow until you have disowned me three times.' (Lk 22:31-34)

Institution of the Eucharist: Jesus is the true lamb of the new covenant

During the meal, Jesus took bread, and blessed it and broke it; and as he gave it to the disciples, he said: 'Take this and eat it; this is my body.'

Then he took a chalice, and offered thanks, and gave it to them saying: 'Drink of this, all of you; for this is my blood, the blood of the Covenant, shed for many for the forgiveness of sins. I tell you, from now I shall not drink this fruit of the vine until the day when I drink new wine with you in my Father's kingdom.' (Mt 26:26-29)

**Only in Jesus
the Master, Way,
Truth and Life,
is there hope
of salvation**

'Do not let your hearts be troubled; have faith in God and faith in me. In my Father's house there is room for many to find their home; if it were not so, I should have told you. For I am going to prepare a place for you. After I have been there and prepared a place for you, I shall come back and take you to myself, so that where I am, you too may be. You know the way to the place where I am going.'

But Thomas said to him: 'Lord, we do not know where you are going; how can we know the way?' Jesus answered: 'I am the way — and the truth and the life; no one comes to the Father except by way of me. If you knew me, you would know my Father too; indeed you do know him now, and have seen him.' Then Philip said: 'Lord, only show us the Father, and we shall be satisfied.' Jesus replied: 'After I have been with you all this time, Philip, do you still not know me? Whoever has seen me has seen the Father. How can you say, "Show us the Father"? Do you not believe that that I am in the Father and the Father is in me? The words that I speak to you are not my own words; and these works — the Father who dwells in me does them himself. Believe my word when I say that I am in the Father and the Father is in me; or at least believe the witness of the very works that I do.

'I tell you truly, he who believes in me will do works such as I do, and even greater. For I am going to the Father, and anything you ask in my name I shall do, in order that my Father may be glorified in his Son. If you ask for anything in my name, I shall do it.'   (Jn 14:1-14)

**The Holy Spirit,
gift of peace
and inner light**

'If you love me, you will keep my commandments, and I shall ask the Father and he will give you another Paraclete, to remain with you for ever — the Spirit of Truth, whom the world cannot receive because it neither sees him nor knows him. You will know him, because he will make his home with you and be in your midst. I shall not leave you orphans; I shall come back to you. A little while and the world will see me no more, but you will see me; for I am living, and you too will live. On that day, you will know that I am in my Father, and you are in me, and I in you. He who has my commandments and keeps them — he is the man who loves me; and he who loves me will be loved by my Father, and I shall love him and reveal myself to him.'

Judas (not the Iscariot, but the other) said to him: 'Lord, how is it that you will reveal yourself to us and not to the world?' In answer Jesus said to him: 'If anyone loves me, he will keep my word, and my Father will love him, and we shall come to him and make our home with him.

'He who does not love me does not keep my words — not that the word which you hear is mine; it is the word of the Father who sent me.

'I have told you all this while still with you; but the Holy Spirit, the Paraclete, whom the Father will send in my name, will explain and bring back to your minds all that I have told you.

'Peace I leave you, my own peace I give you; not such as the world gives is the peace I give you. Do not let your hearts be troubled or dismayed; you have heard me say, "I am going away, but I shall come back to you." If you loved me, you would be glad that I am going to the Father; for the Father is greater than I. I have told you now, before it happens, so that when it does happen, you will believe.

'I shall not say much more to you now; for the ruler of this world is coming. He has no claim on me; but to show the world that I love the Father and do as he has commanded me, rise up, let us go from here.'

(Jn 14:15-31)

The vine and the branches: Jesus shares his life with the disciples

'I am the true Vine, and my Father is the Vinedresser. Those of my branches that do not bear fruit, he cuts off; and those which do bear fruit, he cleans, so that they will yield still more. (You are clean already, by reason of the word that I have spoken to you.) Remain in me, and I shall remain in you. A branch cannot yield its fruit unless it remains on the vine, and no more can you, unless you remain attached to me.

'I am the Vine, you are the branches. The man who remains attached to me, and I to him, he it is who yields fruit in plenty; for apart from me you can do nothing. He who does not remain attached to me, is cast out like a broken branch and withers; and withered branches are gathered up, thrown on the fire and burnt.

'If you remain attached to me, and my words remain in you, ask whatever you wish, and it will be done for you. It is to my Father's glory if you bear fruit in plenty and show yourselves my true disciples.

'As the Father has loved me, so I have loved you. Remain in my love. If you keep my commandments, you will remain in my love, (just as I have kept my Father's commandments and remain in his love). This I have said to you so that my joy may dwell in you, and your joy may be complete.

'This is my commandment: love one another, as I have loved you. There is no greater proof of love than this, that a man lays down his life for his friends. You are my friends, if you do as I command you. I do not say that you are slaves; a slave does not know what his master is doing. I call you my friends because I have made known to you all that I have heard from my Father. It was not you who chose me; it was I who chose you. I have appointed you to go forth and bear fruit, fruit that will last. And whatever you ask the Father in my name he will give you. This is the commandment I give you: You must love one another.' (Jn 15:1-17)

The world will
hate good people
as it has hated
Jesus

'If the world hates you, remember that it hated me before it hated you. If you were of the world, the world would love you as its own; but you are not of the world, because I have chosen you out of the world, and therefore you are hated by the world. Remember my saying, "The servant is not greater than his lord." Have they persecuted me? They will persecute you. Have they heeded my word? No more will they heed yours. They will treat you in this way on account of my name, because they do not know the one who sent me. If I had not come and spoken to them, they would not be guilty; as it is, they have no excuse for their sin. He who hates me, hates my Father too. If I had not done among them works that no one else has ever done, they would not be guilty; as it is, they have seen and hated both me and my Father. However, the words of their Law could not but prove true; it is written that *they have hated me without cause.*

'When the Paraclete comes, whom I shall send you from the Father, he, the Spirit of Truth, who comes forth from the Father, will bear witness about me. And you too will bear me witness; for you have been with me from the beginning.

'I am forewarning you of all this, so that your faith will not be overthrown. You will be excommunicated from the synagogue; indeed the time is coming when the man who kills you will think he is rendering a service to God. They will treat you in this way, because they have known neither the Father nor me. But I am forewarning you of all this, so that when the time comes, you will remember that I warned you.'

(Jn 15:18-27; 16:1-4)

The sin of the
world is its
unbelief; but
evil will not
prevail

'At the beginning I did not tell you of this, because I was with you. But now I am going to him who sent me, and none of you asks me where I am going. Your hearts are filled with grief because I have told you these things. But I tell you the truth: it is for your good that I should leave you, because if I do not go, the Paraclete will not come to you; but if I go, I shall send him to you. He will come and convince the world about sin, about justice, about judgement: about men's sin, that they have sinned by not believing in me; about the justice of my claims, that when you see me no more I go to the Father; about the judgement of this world, that its ruler has been condemned already.

'I still have many things to tell you, which as yet you cannot bear. But when the Spirit of Truth comes, he will guide you into all truth. What he tells you will not be his own; he will tell you the things he has heard, and will declare to you things that are still to come. He will give glory to me, because it is from me that he will receive what he declares to you. All that the Father has is mine; that is why I said that it is from me he will receive what he declares to you.'

(Jn 16:4-15)

Sorrow will turn into joy at the Lord's return

'A little while and you will see me no longer, then another little while and you will see me again.' At this, some of his disciples said to one another: 'What does he mean by saying to us, "A little while and you will see me no longer, then another little while and you will see me again?" And what does he mean by saying, "I am going to the Father?" What is this "little while" that he talks about?' they said; 'we do not know what he means.' Jesus knew that they wanted to question him. So he said to them: 'You are asking one another about my saying, "A little while and you will not see me, then another little while and you will see me again." I tell you truly, soon you will weep and lament, but the world will rejoice. But though you will grieve, your grief will turn into joy. When a woman is in labour, she suffers distress because her hour is come. But when she has given birth to her child, she no longer remembers her pangs, for joy that a man has been born into the world. So too with you: you are distressed at present; but I shall see you again, and your hearts will rejoice, and no one will take away your joy. On that day you will no longer ask anything from me. I tell you truly, if you ask anything from the Father in my name, he will give it to you. Hitherto you have not asked for anything in my name; ask, and you will receive, and so your joy will be complete.'

(Jn 16:16-24)

The faith of believers is founded on Christ who has overcome the world

'I have told you these things in parables, but a time is coming when I shall no longer speak to you in parables, but tell you plainly about the Father. On that day, you will make your requests in my name. I do not mean that I shall speak to the Father on your behalf; the Father himself loves you — because you have loved me and have believed that I came from God. I came from the Father and have come into the world; now I am leaving the world and going back to the Father.'

His disciples said: 'But already you are talking plainly and speaking no parable! Already we know that you know everything, and that there is no need for anyone to ask you anything. At this present time we believe that you came from God.' Jesus replied: 'You now believe? I tell you, the hour is coming, and indeed has come, when you will all be scattered, each on his own, and will leave me deserted. Yet I shall not be alone: for the Father is with me. I have told you all this so that you will find peace in me. In this world you have tribulations. But courage! I have conquered the world.'

(Jn 16:25-33)

Jesus prayed that if it were possible the hour might pass away from him. He kept saying: 'Abba! Father! All things are possible to you; take this chalice away from me! Yet not what I will, but what you will'

**Jesus'
priestly prayer
in the hour
of sacrifice**

After Jesus had said this, he raised his eyes to heaven and prayed: 'Father, the hour is come! Glorify your Son, that your Son may glorify you, that by the popwer which you have given him over all mankind he may give eternal life to all whom you have given him. (This is eternal life: to know you who are the one true God and Jesus Christ whom you have sent.) I have glorified you on earth by completing the work which you gave me to do. And now, Father, glorify me at your side with the glory which I had with you before the world began.

'I have manifested your Name to the men whom you have drawn from the world and given me. They were yours, you gave them to me, and they have kept your word. Now they know that all I have is from you, and is your gift; for I have given them the words which you gave to me, and they have received them; they have learned to know in truth that I came forth from you, and to believe that it was you who sent me.'   (Jn 17:1-8)

**Prayer for
the disciples,
that their joy
may be complete**

'For them I pray, not for the world, but for these whom you have given me; for they belong to you; all that is mine is yours, and yours is mine; and I am glorified in them. They are in the world, but I am no longer in the world, I am on my way to you. Holy Father, keep them in your Name, these whom you gave me, that they may be one, as we are one. So long as I was with them, I watched over them in your Name, which you gave me; I protected them, and none of them perished, except the one who is destined to be lost, for the Scripture must be fulfilled. Now I am on my way to you; but while I am still in the world, I speak these words; in order that they may have my joy in their hearts in full measure. I have given them your word. The world has come to hate them, because they are not of the world, as I am not of the world. I do not ask that you would take them out of the world, but that you would keep them safe from the evil one. They are not of the world, as I am not of the world. Consecrate them in the truth, the truth which is your word. As you sent me into the world, so I have sent them into the world. And for their sake I consecrate myself, that they too may be consecrated in the truth.'   (Jn 17:9-19)

**Prayer for
the Church, that
all the faithful
may be perfect
in unity**

'Not for these alone do I pray but for those too who through their word will believe in me: may they all be one; may they too be in us, as you, Father, in me and I in you, that the world may believe that it was you who sent me. The glory which you gave me, I have given to them, that they may be one, as we are one. I in them, and you in me, that they may be perfectly one, that the world may know that it was you who sent me, and that you have loved them as you loved me.

'Father, my prayer for these whom you have given me is that where I am going to be, they too may be with me, that they may see the glory which you gave me, because you loved me, before the world's creation. Merciful Father, the world has not known you, but I have known you, and these men have learned to know that it was you who sent me. I have revealed and shall reveal your Name to them, so that the love with which you have loved me may be in them, and I too in them.' (Jn 17:20-26)

GOOD FRIDAY: THE PASSION OF THE LORD

The agony of Gethsemane

They arrived at a place called Gethsemane, and Jesus said to his disciples: 'Sit down here, while I pray.' But he took with him Peter and James and John. Then he began to feel deep anguish and distress, and he said to them: '*My heart is* ready to break *with grief*. Stay here and keep watch.' Then he went forward a little and fell on the ground, and prayed that if it were possible the hour might pass away from him. He kept saying: 'Abba! Father! All things are possible to you; take this chalice away from me! Yet not what I will, but what you will.' Then he came and found the three disciples sleeping, and he said to Peter: 'Simon, are you sleeping? Could you not keep watch even for one hour? Watch and pray that you may not yield to temptation. The spirit indeed is willing, but the flesh is weak.' Again he went away and prayed, using the same words; and again he came back and found the disciples sleeping, for their eyes were heavy; and they did not know what to say to him. And he came a third time, and said to them: 'Sleep on now, and take your rest! . . . Enough! The hour has come; see, the Son of Man is betrayed into the hands of sinners! Rise up, let us go. My betrayer is at hand!'

(Mk 14:32-42)

Jesus is God ("I am") and willingly accepts his passion

Judas, his betrayer, also knew the place, because Jesus and his disciples had often gathered there. So Judas took with him a detachment of soldiers, and also some servants given him by the chief priests and Pharisees, and came to the place with lanterns, torches and weapons. Jesus knew well all that awaited him; nevertheless he went forward and said to them: 'Who is it you are looking for?' They replied: 'Jesus of Nazareth.' Jesus said to them: '*I am* he.' (Judas, his betrayer, was standing there with them.) When Jesus said to them: '*I am* he,' they recoiled and fell to the ground. So again he asked them: 'Who is it you are looking for?' and they replied: 'Jesus of Nazareth.' Jesus answered: 'I have told you that *I am* he; if *I am* the one you are looking for, allow these others to go.' And so the words of his prayer remained true: 'I have not lost one of those whom you have given me.' Then Simon Peter, who had a sword, struck at a servant of the High Priest, and cut off his right ear. (The servant's name was Malchus.) But Jesus said to Peter: 'Sheathe your sword! Shall I not drink the chalice which my Father has given me?'

(Jn 18:2-11)

**Judas betrays Jesus
with a kiss.
All desert him**

At that moment, while he was still speaking, Judas, one of the Twelve, arrived and with him a crowd of men armed with swords and truncheons, sent by the chief priests and the scribes and the elders. The traitor had arranged a signal with them: 'The one I kiss,' he had said, 'that is the man; hold him fast and watch how you take him away!' When he appeared, he went straight to Jesus, greeted him as 'Rabbi', and gave him a kiss. Then they seized Jesus and held him. (One of those standing at his side drew his sword and struck at a servant of the High Priest and cut off one of his ears.) Then Jesus spoke: 'Am I a brigand that you come out with swords and truncheons to arrest me? Day by day I have been with you in the temple teaching, and you did not arrest me then. However, let the Scriptures be fulfilled!' Then all his disciples deserted him and ran away.

One young man began to follow Jesus. He was seized, but as he was wearing nothing but a linen wrap, he slipped out of the wrap and escaped from his captors naked.

(Mk 14:43-52)

**Jesus is questioned
in the house of Annas
and denied by Peter**

Then the soldiers and their officer and the servants of the Jews arrested Jesus, and put him in bonds.

They took him first to Annas, who was the father-in-law of Caiaphas the High Priest of that year. It was Caiaphas who had advised the Jews that it was necessary that one man should die for the people.

Simon Peter and another disciple were following Jesus. This other disciple was known to the High Priest, and went with Jesus into the High Priest's courtyard; but Peter stopped outside, near the door. So the other disciple, the one who was known to the High Priest, went out and spoke to the girl who was doorkeeper, and she let Peter in. She said to Peter: 'Are you another of this man's disciples?' He replied: 'No, I am not.' As it was cold, the slaves and servants had made a fire, and were standing round it, warming themselves; and Peter was warming himself with them.

The High Priest questioned Jesus about his disciples and about his teaching. Jesus replied: 'I have spoken openly to the world. I have always taught in the synagogue and in the temple, where all the Jews foregather, and I have said nothing in secret. Why do you question me? Ask my hearers what I have said to them. Why, these people here know what I said!' At this reply, one of the servants standing near gave Jesus a blow: 'Is that how you answer the High Priest?' he asked. Jesus replied: 'If I have said anything wrong, bring it as evidence against me. If not, why do you strike me?' Then Annas sent Jesus, still in bonds, to the High Priest Caiaphas.

Simon Peter was still standing there warming himself with the others. They said to him: 'Are you not one of his disciples?' He denied it: 'No, I am not,' he said. Then one of the High Priest's servants said to him (he was a kinsman of the one whose ear Peter had cut off): 'I saw you with him in the garden, did I not?' Peter again denied it; and at once a cock crew. The Lord turned and looked at Peter. Peter remembered the word which the Lord had said to him: 'Before the cock has crowed tomorrow, you will deny me three times.' And he went outside and wept bitterly.

(Jn 18:12-27; Jn 22:61-62)

The religious trial: Jesus is condemned as a blasphemer

They took Jesus to the High Priest, at whose house the chief priests and the elders and the scribes were gathering.

Peter had followed Jesus, at a distance, right into the courtyard of the High Priest's house, and was sitting with the guards, warming himself at the fire.

The chief priests and the whole Sanhedrin sought evidence against Jesus on which to send him to his death, but they did not find anything. Many witnesses gave testimony against him, but they were lying, and their evidence did not agree. Among them were some who stood up and falsely testified against him, that they had heard him say, 'I shall demolish this temple made with hands, and in three days build up another not made with hands.' But even here their evidence was contradictory.

Then the High Priest stood up in full view and questioned Jesus: 'Have you no answer,' he said, 'to the charges made against you?' But Jesus remained silent and gave no answer, until the High Priest put another question to him: 'Are you the Messiah, the Son of the Blessed One?' And Jesus said: '*I am! And you will see the Son of Man seated at the right of the Almighty and coming with the clouds of heaven.*' At this the High Priest tore his clothes and cried: 'What need have we any more of witnesses? You yourselves have heard the blasphemy; what is your verdict?' They declared him guilty and condemned him to death.

Then some of them spat on him and blindfolded him and struck him, saying: 'Play the prophet!' And the guards too gave him blows as they took him away.

(Mk 14:53-65)

Judas, desperate because he is a traitor, kills himself

When Judas, who had betrayed him, saw that Jesus had been condemned, he was stricken with remorse. He took back the thirty silver pieces to the chief priests and elders, and cried: 'I have sinned; I have betrayed an innocent man.' They retorted: 'What has that to do with us? It is your concern!' Then he flung down the silver pieces, left the temple, and went away and hanged himself. When the chief priests recovered the silver pieces they said: 'It is not lawful to put the money into the treasury, since it is the price of blood.' After some discussion, they used it to buy the Potter's Field, to serve as a burial ground for foreigners. That is why to this day it goes by the name of "The Field of Blood". Then was fulfilled the word spoken by the prophet Jeremiah, when he said: *And they took the thirty silver pieces, the small price set upon the most prized of the sons of Israel, and bought with them the Potter's Field, as the Lord had bidden me.* (Mt 27:3-10)

The civil trial: Jesus is accused as a rebel

It was now early morning. From the house of Caiaphas they took Jesus to the governor's palace; but they did not enter the palace, lest they should incur defilement and be unable to eat the Passover. Pilate, therefore, came out to them. 'What charge,' he asked, 'do you bring against this man?' They replied: 'If he were not a criminal, we should hardly have handed him over to you!' So Pilate said to them: 'You take him then, and deal with him by your law!' The Jews replied: 'We are not allowed to put anyone to death.' So it came about that Jesus' prophecy about the manner of his death was fulfilled.

Then Pilate went back into the palace. He summoned Jesus, and said to him: 'So you are the king of the Jews?' Jesus answered: 'Is this question your own, or is it what others have told you about me?' Pilate replied: 'Am I a Jew? Your own people and the chief priests have handed you over to me. What have you done?' Jesus replied: 'My kingdom is not of this world; if my kingdom were of this world, soldiers of mine would be fighting to save me from falling into the hands of the Jews. As it is, my kingdom is not of this world.' Pilate exclaimed: 'So you are a king then?' Jesus replied: 'If you put it so, I am a king. I was born and I came into the world for this one purpose: to bear witness to the truth. All who are on the side of truth heed my voice.' Pilate replied: 'What is truth?' — and with that, he went out again to the Jews and said to them: 'I find him not guilty'. (Jn 18:28-38)

Jesus, prophet of Galilee, is scorned by Herod Antipas

Pilate said to the chief priests and the people: 'I do not find this man guilty of any crime.' But they insisted: 'He has been spreading disaffection among the people by his teaching, from Galilee all through Judea and now here.'

When Pilate heard this, he asked: 'Is the man a Galilean?' and learning that he belonged to Herod's jurisdiction, he referred the case to Herod, who was in Jerusalem at the time. Herod was greatly pleased to see Jesus. He had long been wanting to see him because of all that he had heard about him; and he was hoping to see a miracle worked by him. He put many questions to him; but Jesus gave him no answer, although the chief priests and the scribes continued to stand there accusing him remorselessly. So Herod and his bodyguard treated him with contempt and made a mockery of him, and sent him back to Pilate dressed up in a gorgeous robe. That very day Herod and Pilate became friends, whereas previously they had been at enmity.

(Lk 23:4-12)

Pilate suggests the infamous choice with the rogue Barabbas

During the festival, it was usual for the governor to grant the release of a prisoner chosen by the people. At this time a notorious prisoner called Barabbas was held in gaol. So when the people assembled, Pilate said to them: 'Which of them do you want me to release for you, Barabbas, or Jesus who is called the Christ?' For he knew that it was from jealousy that Jesus had been handed over. While Pilate was seated on the rostrum, his wife sent him a message: 'Do nothing against that innocent man;' she said, ' I suffered much in a dream last night on account of him.'

But the chief priests and elders urged the crowd to ask for the release of Barabbas and to have Jesus put to death. The governor addressed them and said: 'Which of the two do you want me to release for you?' They cried: 'Barabbas!' Pilate said to them: 'Then what am I to do with Jesus, the one called Christ?' They all cried: 'Crucify him!' He said: 'Why? What crime has he committed?' But they shouted still louder: 'Crucify him!'

As Pilate saw that it was useless and the tumult was growing, he had water fetched, and washed his hands before the crowd. 'I am innocent of shedding this man's blood;' he said, 'it is your responsibility.' All the people answered: 'His blood be on us and our children!' Then Pilate released Barabbas for them [. . .].

(Mt 27:15-26)

Pilate, through cowardice, condemns the innocent Jesus to scourging and death on the cross

Then Pilate took Jesus and had him scourged. The soldiers plaited a crown of thorns and placed it on his head, and dressed him up in a purple cloak: then they came before him and said: 'Hail, king of the Jews!' and struck him. Afterwards, Pilate went out again and said to the Jews: 'Look! I am bringing him out to you, and I would have you know that I find him not guilty.' Jesus came outside, wearing the crown of thorns and the purple cloak; and Pilate said to them: 'Here is the Man!' When the chief priests and their servants saw him they shouted out: 'Crucify him! Crucify him!' Pilate said to them: 'Take him and crucify him yourselves. I find him not guilty.' The Jews replied: 'We have a law, and according to our law he must die, because he claimed to be God's Son.' When Pilate heard this, he was still more alarmed. He went back into the palace and said to Jesus: 'Where do you come from?' But Jesus did not give him an answer. Pilate said to him: 'You refuse to speak to me? Do you know that I have power to release you, and power to crucify you?' Jesus replied: 'You would not have any power against me, had it not been granted you from above. The sin of the man who handed me over to you is so much the graver for that.' From this point, Pilate wanted to release Jesus; but the Jews kept shouting: 'If you release him, you are no friend of Caesar; anyone who claims to be a king is setting himself against Caesar.' When Pilate heard this, he brought Jesus out to the place called "Lithostrotos" (or in Hebrew "Gabbatha"), and made him sit down on the rostrum. It was the Eve of the Passover, about mid-day. Pilate said to the Jews: 'Here is your king!' They shouted: 'Away with him! Crucify him!' Pilate said to them: 'Am I to crucify your king?' The chief priests replied: 'We have no king but Caesar.' Then he yielded to them and gave Jesus up to be crucified.

So Jesus was given into their charge. He went out, carrying his own cross, to the place called in Hebrew "Golgotha", that is "the place of the Skull", where they crucified him.

(Jn 19:1-17)

Simon of Cyrene helps Jesus to carry the cross. Lament of the women

As they were leading him away, they stopped a certain Simon of Cyrene, who was coming in from the country, and put the cross on his shoulder to carry behind Jesus.

A great throng of the people followed him, and many women, who beat their breasts and wept for him. Jesus turned to them and said: 'Daughters of Jerusalem, do not weep for me. Weep for yourselves and for your children. For the days are coming when people will say, "Happy are the childless, the wombs that have not borne a child, and the breasts that have not suckled!" Then *they will say to the mountains: "Fall on us!", and to the hills: "Bury us"*. For if this can happen to the green wood, what will become of the dry?' Two others were led out with him, criminals to be put to death.

(Lk 23:26-32)

Jesus, crucified between two criminals, pardons those who have crucified him and the penitent thief

When they came to the place called "Calvary", they crucified him there, with the criminals one on his right and one on his left. Jesus prayed: 'Father, forgive them; they know not what they do.' Then they divided his clothes and cast lots for them.

The people stood there looking on, and the rulers sneered at him. 'He saved others,' they said, 'now let him save himself, if he is God's Anointed and Chosen One!' The soldiers too joined in the mockery, as they came up and offered him vinegar. They too said: 'If you are the King of the Jews, save yourself!' Over his head was the inscription: "This is the King of the Jews."

One of the criminals hanged there jeered at him: 'Are you not the Messiah?' he said. 'Then if you are, save yourself — and us!' But the other criminal broke in and rebuked him: 'Do you not even fear God, when you are under the same sentence? Our sentence at least is just: we are only getting what our crimes deserved: but this man has done nothing wrong.' Then he said: 'Jesus, remember me when you come with your royal power!' Jesus replied: 'I tell you truly, this very day you shall be with me in paradise.'

(Lk 23:33-43)

Jesus, the Crucified King, entrusts his mother to John thus making her Mother of the Church

Pilate also had written and fastened on the cross a title which bore the words: "Jesus of Nazareth, the King of the Jews". Many of the Jews read this, because the place where Jesus was crucified was close to the city, and the writing was in Hebrew, Latin and Greek. So the chief priests of the Jews asked Pilate if, instead of "The King of the Jews", he would write "This man claimed to be King of the Jews." But Pilate replied: 'What I have written, I have written.'

After the soldiers had crucified Jesus, they took his clothes and divided them into four parts, one for each soldier. There was also his cloak, but as it was seamless, woven in one piece from top to bottom, they agreed among themselves that they would not tear it, but would cast lots to see whose it should be. Thus the Scripture was fulfilled which says: *They divided my garments among them and cast lots for my clothing.*

While the soldiers were doing this, beside the cross of Jesus stood his mother, and his mother's sister, Mary the wife of Clopas, and Mary Magdalene. When Jesus saw his mother and the disciple whom he loved standing by her, he said to his mother: 'Woman, there is your son.' Then he said to the disciple: 'There is your mother.' And from that hour the disciple took her into his care.

(Jn 19:19-27)

**Jesus,
the redeemer,
dies on the cross
to save the world**

From midday onwards, darkness covered all the land until three. About three o'clock, Jesus cried out in a loud voice: '*Eli, Eli, lama sabachtani,*' that is, '*My God, my God, why have you forsaken me?*' Some of the bystanders heard this and said: 'He is calling Elijah!' One of them at once ran and fetched a sponge, and soaked it in vinegar, fixed it on a cane and held it up for Jesus to drink. But the rest said: 'Wait! Let us see if Elijah comes to save him!'

After this, when Jesus knew that all was now over, wishing to bring about the fulfilment of a prophecy, he cried out: '*I thirst.*' There was a vessel of sharp wine standing there; so a sponge was steeped in the wine, placed on a spear, and put to his mouth. Jesus took the wine, and said: 'All is over!' Then he bowed his head, and gave up the spirit.

(Mt 27:45-49; Jn 19:28-30)

**The old covenant,
pictured in the
temple, is ended**

Suddenly, the curtain of the temple was rent in two from top to bottom; the earth shook, rocks were rent, graves were opened; and the bodies of many saints who had gone to their rest rose up (they came out of their graves after his resurrection, and entered the holy city and were seen by many). The centurion and the men who were with him on guard over Jesus saw the earthquake and all that was happening, and were greatly frightened; and they exclaimed: 'He was indeed God's Son!'

Watching from a distance were some women who had accompanied Jesus from Galilee to minister to his needs. Among them were Mary Magdalene, Mary the mother of James and Joseph, and the mother of the sons of Zebedee.

(Mt 27:51-56)

Jesus, true lamb of the new Passover, is pierced in his side

It was the eve of the Passover, and the Jews, who did not wish the bodies to be still hanging on the crosses on the next day, which was both the sabbath and the great feast day, obtained permission from Pilate to have the legs broken and the bodies taken away. The soldiers, therefore, came and broke the legs of the first man and then of the other who had been crucified with him. But when they came to Jesus, they saw that he was already dead, and did not break his legs, but one of the soldiers stabbed his side with a spear, and at once blood and water poured out. This is vouched for by one who saw it happen, whose witness is trustworthy, and who knows that he is telling the truth, so that you too may believe. For these things happened in fulfilment of the text of Scripture which says: *You shall not break any of his bones*, and likewise of another text which says: *They will look on him whom they have pierced.*

(Jn 19:31-37)

SATURDAY IN HOLY WEEK

Jesus is hurriedly buried, wrapped in a shroud. The great week ends in the peace of the tomb

When evening came, because it was the day of preparation (that is, the eve of the sabbath), Joseph of Arimathea, who was a councillor and a man of position and was moreover looking forward to the coming of God's kingdom, courageously went into Pilate and asked for the body of Jesus. Pilate was surprised that he should be dead already. So he sent for the centurion and asked whether he had been dead for some time. On receiving the centurion's assurance, he granted the body to Joseph without payment. Joseph bought a linen shroud, and took Jesus down and wrapped him in it. Then he laid him in a tomb cut out of a rock, and rolled a stone against the doorway of the tomb. Mary Magdalene and Mary the mother of Jesus observed where he was laid.

On the next day (the one following the day of preparation), the chief priests and the Pharisees went in a body to Pilate, and said: 'Sir, we have remembered that while that imposter was still alive, he said: "After three days I shall arise." Pray give orders, therefore, for the tomb to be made secure during the next three days, or his disciples may go and steal the body and tell the people that he has risen from the dead; then the last imposture will be worse than the first.' Pilate replied: 'You are granted a guard; go and take whatever measures you think fit.' They went and made the tomb secure, by sealing the stone and setting the guard.

(Mk 15:42-47; Mt 27:62-66)

fter the sabbath was over, towards dawn on the first day of the week [...] suddenly the earth quaked violently; for an angel of the Lord came down from heaven. He went to the tomb, rolled away the stone, and seated himself upon it, his face bright as lightening, his dress white as snow. The guards trembled in awe of him and became like dead men.

(Mt 28:1-4)

The first day of the new creation: the empty tomb

When the sabbath was over, Mary Magdalene, Mary the mother of James, and Salome bought spices to go and anoint him. Very early on the first day of the week, after the sun had risen, they went to the tomb. They were asking one another who would roll away the stone for them from the entrance of the tomb, when they looked and saw that the stone, a large one, was rolled back already. Entering the tomb, they saw a young man sitting on the right side, dressed in a white robe, and they were seized with amazement. But he said to them: 'Do not be amazed. You are looking for Jesus of Nazareth who was crucified. He has been raised up; he is not here. Look, there is the place where he was laid! Go now, and say to Peter and the other disciples: "Jesus is going ahead of you into Galilee, and you will see him there, as he told you".' The women came out of the tomb and ran away, for they were seized with trembling and amazement. And they told nobody anything, because they were afraid. (Mk 16:1-8)

Mary of Magdala, the pardoned sinner, is the first messenger of the resurrection

Early in the morning on the first day of the week, while it was still dark, Mary Magdalene went to the tomb and saw that the stone had been moved away. So she went running to Simon Peter and to the other disciple whom Jesus loved, and said to them: 'They have taken the Lord away from the tomb, and we do not know where they have laid him.' So Peter and the other disciple went out and made for the tomb.

They set off at a run together, but the other disciple ran faster than Peter, and reached the tomb first. He bent down and saw the linen cloths lying there, and noticed that the veil which had covered his head was not lying with the linen cloths, but folded up separately in a place by itself. Then the other disciple, who had been the first to reach the tomb, also went and he saw and believed. (Until then they had not understood the Scriptures which said that he must rise from the dead.)

The disciples then went back to their lodging, but Mary stayed there, weeping, outside the tomb. Still weeping, she bent down and looked inside the tomb; and she saw two angels in white sitting where the body of Jesus had lain, one at the head and one at the feet. They said to her: 'Woman, why are you weeping?' She replied: 'Because they have taken my Lord away, and I do not know where they have laid him.' As she said this, she turned away; and she saw Jesus standing there, but did not know it was Jesus. He said to her: 'Woman, why are you weeping? Who is it you are looking for?' Thinking it was the gardener, she said to him: 'Sir, if it was you who moved him, tell me where you have laid him, and I will take him away.' Jesus said to her: 'Mary!' She turned and cried out: 'Rabboni!' (which is Hebrew for "Master"). Jesus said to her: 'Do not cling to me — I still have not ascended to the Father! Go to my brethren and tell them: "I am on my way up to him who is my Father and your Father, my God and your God."' Mary Magdalene went and announced to the disciples: 'I have seen the Lord!' And she told them what he had said to her.

(Jn 20:1-18)

The risen Jesus appears to the women. Bribery of the guards

The women went quickly away from the tomb, in fear — but also in great joy, and broke into a run in order to tell his disciples. Suddenly, there was Jesus in front of them, greeting them! They rushed forward, clasped his feet, and worshipped him. Then Jesus said to them: 'Do not be afraid; go and tell my brothers to leave for Galilee, where they will see me.'

While they were going, some of the guard went into the city and reported to the chief priests all that had happened. These met with the elders, and after a discussion, offered the soldiers a large sum of money and said to them: 'Tell people that his disciples came by night and stole his body while you were asleep; if the governor hears of the matter, we will speak to him and see that you have no cause for worry'.

The soldiers accepted the money and did as they had been told; and so this explanation has been put about among the Jews from that day to this.

(Mt 28:8-15)

Jesus teaches the Emmaus disciples to read the Bible in the light of the resurrection

On the same day, two of them were walking to a village called Emmaus about seven miles from Jerusalem, and were talking to each other about all these events. Jesus himself came up, in the middle of their talk and discussion, and walked along with them; but their eyes were not allowed to recognise him. He said to them: 'What is it you are arguing about as you walk along?' They stood still, with faces downcast, and one of them (his name was Clopas) exclaimed: 'If you did not hear what happened in Jerusalem in these last few days, you were the only man in the city who did not!' He said to them: 'What did happen?' They said: 'Why, the affair of Jesus of Nazareth — a prophet who was mighty in word and deed before God and all the people. We ourselves had hopes that it was he who would deliver Israel, until our chief priests and rulers gave him up to be condemned to death, and then crucified him. And another thing, it is now the third day since all this happened, and some of our womenfolk have told us an alarming story: they went to the tomb at day-break, found that his body was not there, and came back claiming to have seen a vision of angels, who said that he is alive. Some of our people then went to the tomb and found everything just as the women had said, but they did not see Jesus himself.'

'How foolish you are!' Jesus replied. 'How slow you have been to believe all that the prophets foretold! Was it not necessary that the Messiah should suffer before entering into his glory?' Then he began from Moses and went through all the prophets explaining to them all the texts referring to himself.

When they came to the village where they were going to stay, Jesus made as if to go further; but they would not let him. 'Stay with us,' they said, 'for it is evening, and the day is far advanced.' So he went in to stay with them. While he was sitting with them at table, he took bread and blessed and broke it and gave it to them. Then their eyes were opened and they recognised him; but he became invisible to them. They said to each other: 'Were not our minds under a veil while he was speaking to us on the road and expounding the Scriptures to us?' At once they started up and returned to Jerusalem, where they were greeted by the Eleven and the other disciples, who had all assembled, with the cry: 'It is true! The Lord has risen. He has appeared to Simon.' Then they told their story about what had happened on their journey and how they had recognised Jesus in the breaking of bread.

(Lk 24:13-35)

Jesus appears to the disciples so that they may become witnesses of the resurrection

While they were still talking about all this, Jesus stood in the middle of them and said: 'Peace be upon you!' But panic and fear seized them, for they thought they were seeing a ghost. Jesus said to them: 'Why this confusion? Why do these doubts spring up in your hearts? Look at my hands and my feet and see that it is myself!

178

Touch me and see — a ghost has no flesh or bones as you see that I have.' With this, he showed them his hands and feet. Then, as they were so overjoyed and astonished that they still could not bring themselves to believe it, he said to them: 'Have you anything here to eat?' They gave him a piece of roasted fish, which he took and ate before their eyes.

Then he said to them: 'This is what I meant when I said to you while I was still with you, that everything written about me in the Law of Moses and in the prophets and the psalms must be fulfilled.' Then he opened their minds to understand the Scriptures. 'This,' he said, 'is what the Scriptures say: the Messiah must suffer, but three days later he will rise from the dead, and in his name repentance for the forgiveness of sins is to be proclaimed to all the nations, beginning from Jerusalem. You are the witnesses of these events. See, I am about to send upon you the Father's promised Gift; you must remain in the city until you are clothed with power from on high.'

Then Jesus said again: 'Peace be with you!' and he added: 'As the Father sent me, so I send you.' Then he breathed on them and said: 'Receive the Holy Spirit; those whose sins you absolve, are absolved from their sins; those whose sins you retain, remain in their sins.'

(Lk 24:36-49; Jn 20:21-23)

Thomas' doubt: blessed are those who believe on the word of witness without being witnesses themselves

Now one of the Twelve, Thomas (also called "the Twin"), had not been with the other disciples when Jesus came; and when they said to him: 'We have seen the Lord!' he replied: 'Unless I see the marks of the nails in his hands, and put my finger into the place where the nails were, and my hand into his side, I will not believe.'

A week later, the disciples were again inside, and Thomas was with them. Although the doors were locked, Jesus came in and stood among them. He said: 'Peace be with you!' then turned to Thomas: 'Come,' he said, 'where is your finger? Feel my hands. Where is your hand? Put it into my side. Set aside your doubts and believe.' Thomas answered: 'My Lord and my God!' Jesus said: 'Do you believe because you have seen me? Blessed are those who have not seen and yet believe.'   (Jn 20:24-29)

Jesus appears
to the disciples
in Galilee
on the lake of
Gennesaret
(or Tiberias)

On a later occasion, Jesus showed himself to his disciples at the Sea of Tiberias. This is how it happened. Simon Peter, Thomas (also called "the Twin"), Nathanael from Cana in Galilee, the sons of Zebedee, and two more of his disciples were together, and Simon Peter said: 'I am going fishing.' The others replied: 'We will come with you.' So they went out and boarded the boat, and all that night they caught nothing.

Dawn was already breaking, when Jesus came and stood on the shore; but the disciples did not know that it was Jesus. He called to them: 'Have you any fish, my friends?' They replied: 'No!' He said to them: 'Cast your net out to the right of the boat, and see what you find.' They did as he said, and so great was the catch of fish that they had not enough strength to pull in the net. Then the disciple whom Jesus loved said to Peter: 'It is the Lord!' When Simon Peter heard that it was the Lord, he tucked up his tunic (he had nothing else on) and jumped into the sea. The other disciples came to land in the boat, dragging the net full of fish; for they were not far out, less than a hundred yards from land. When they came ashore, they saw a fire on the beach, with fish cooking on it, and some bread. Jesus said to them: 'Fetch some of the fish you have just caught.' So Simon Peter went back and dragged the net to land, loaded with a hundred and fifty three big fish; and although there were so many, the net did not break. Jesus said to them: 'Come and have breakfast.' None of the disciples ventured to ask him who he was; they knew he was the Lord. Jesus came and took the bread and gave it to them, and so too with the fish. This was the third time that Jesus appeared to the disciples after he had been raised from the dead. (Jn 21:1-14)

Jesus confirms
the penitent Peter
in the primacy
of the Church

When they had finished breakfast, Jesus said to Simon Peter: 'Simon son of John, do you love me more than these others?' He replied: 'Yes, Lord; you know that I love you.' Jesus said to him: 'Feed my lambs.' Then he asked him a second time: 'Simon son of John, do you love me?' Peter replied: 'Yes, Lord; you know that I love you.' Jesus said to him: 'Be the shepherd of my sheep.' Then he asked him a third time: 'Simon son of John, do you love me?' Peter was pained that he asked him this a third time, and he said to Jesus: 'Lord, you know everything; you know that I love you!' Jesus said to him: 'Feed my sheep'.

'I tell you truly, when you were young, you used to tie up your girdle and go off wherever you wished. But when you are old, you will stretch out your hands and another will tie you up and take you off where you do not wish to go.' By these words he signified the manner of death by which Peter was to give glory to God. Then he added: 'Follow me.' Peter was doing so, when he turned round and saw following them the disciple whom Jesus loved; the one who had leaned back on his breast during the supper and asked: 'Lord, who is it that will betray you?' When Peter saw him he said to Jesus: 'Lord, what of him?' Jesus said to Peter: 'If I want him to wait till I come, what is that to you? But for yourself, follow me!' That is the origin of the report which has become current among the brethren that this disciple will not die. But Jesus did not say to Peter: 'He will not die.' He said: 'If I want him to wait till I come, what is that to you?'

(Jn 21:15-23)

Jesus entrusts his mission to the apostles, promising to be with them till the end of the world

The eleven disciples made the journey to Galilee, to the mountain where Jesus had told them to meet him. When they saw him they worshipped him, though some remained in doubt. Then Jesus drew near and addressed them: 'All power has been given to me in heaven and on earth,' he said.

'Go then, and convert all the nations; baptize them in the name of the Father and of the Son and of the Holy Spirit; and teach them to observe all the commandments I have given you. And be sure, I am with you always, even to the end of the world.'

(Mt 28:16-20)

Jesus ascends to heaven, promising the disciples the consoling Spirit

After his Passion, he showed them many proofs that he was still alive; he appeared to them several times over a period of forty days, and spoke to them of the kingdom of God. While sharing a meal with them, he told them not to go away from Jerusalem: 'Wait here,' he said, 'for the fulfilment of the Father's promise which you heard from my lips when I said, "John's baptism was with water, but you will be baptized with the Holy Spirit." It will be fulfilled within a few days from now.'

Once when they were with him, they asked him: 'Lord, is this the time when you will restore the kingdom to Israel?' He answered: 'It is not for you to know the periods and the turning-points of history; the Father has reserved them in his own power. But you are about to receive the power of the Holy Spirit coming upon you; and you are to be my witnesses in Jerusalem, throughout Judea and Samaria, and to the ends of the earth.'

After saying this, he was lifted up before them, until a cloud took him out of their sight. They were straining their eyes looking upwards as he went into heaven, when suddenly two men appeared beside them in white garments. They said: 'Men of Galilee, why are you standing there looking up into heaven? This Jesus, who has just been taken up from you into heaven, will come back in the same way as you have seen him go.'

From Mount Olivet, as the place was called — it is close to Jerusalem, a sabbath's journey distant — they turned back towards the city. They went in, and made their way to the upstairs room where they were lodging: Peter and John, and James and Andrew, Philip and Thomas, Bartholomew and Matthew, James son of Alphaeus and Simon the Zealot, and Judas son of James. All these with one accord devoted themselves to prayer, in union with Mary the mother of Jesus and some other women, and his brethren.

(Acts 1:3-14)

The mission of the apostles continues in the Church. Choice of Matthias

About this time, Peter rose before the assembled brethren, who numbered in all about a hundred and twenty, and said: 'Brethren, through the mouth of David the Holy Spirit spoke a prophecy about Judas, who acted as guide to those who arrested Jesus. This Scripture must now be fulfilled. Judas was one of our number, and received a share in this ministry of ours. (He bought a piece of land with the wages of his crime, and he swelled up, and his belly split and all his entrails poured out. All Jerusalem heard of this, and the piece of land came to be known as "Field of Blood", or in their language "Haceldama".) Now in the Book of Psalms it stands written: *Let his dwelling be desolate; let no one dwell in it;* and again, *let another receive his office.*

'Therefore one of the men who were in our company throughout the public ministry of the Lord Jesus, from the time of John's baptism to the day when he was taken up from us, must be joined to us as a witness of his resurrection.' Two men were put forward: Joseph Barsabbas (also called Justus) and Matthias, and this prayer was made: 'O Lord, the reader of all men's hearts, reveal to us which of these two you have chosen to take his place in this office of ministry and apostleship, from which Judas departed to go to the place where he belonged. Then they threw lots, and the lot fell to Matthias, who was thus appointed apostle along with the other eleven.

(Acts 1:15-26)

On the day of Pentecost, feast of the Law of Sinai, the Holy Spirit gives life to the Church, the new people of God

The day of Pentecost arrived and they were all gathered in one place, when suddenly there came from heaven a sound like the rush of a violent wind, which filled the whole house where they were sitting. And they saw what seemed to be fire separating out into tongues, and settling on each one of them. They were all filled with the Holy Spirit, and began to speak in various languages, as the Spirit granted them power.

Living in Jerusalem there were devout Jews from every nation under heaven. When this sound was heard, they came together in large numbers, and were bewildered because each of them heard the apostles speaking in his own language. They were beside themselves with amazement and asked: 'Are not all these men Galileans, who are speaking? How then is it that each of us hears his own native language? Parthians, Medes and Elamites; men from Mesopotamia, Judea and Cappadocia; from Pontus and Asia, Phrygia and Pamphilia; from Egypt and Cyrenaica; visitors from Rome, both Jews and proselytes; Cretans too and Arabs, all of us hear these men proclaiming God's mighty works in our own languages!'

(Acts 2:1-11)

The age of the Church begins. The Gospel continues through the centuries

After saying all this to them, the Lord Jesus was taken up into heaven and took his seat at God's right hand. They went forth and preached everywhere, and the Lord supported them and confirmed the word by the signs that accompanied them.

Jesus performed many other signs in the presence of his disciples, which are not set down in this book. If they were all recorded in full, I doubt if the whole world would be big enough to hold all the books that would be written. This much has been written down, so that you may believe that Jesus is the Christ, the Son of God, and that through holding this faith you may have life in his name.

(Mk 16:19-20; Jn 20:30-31; 21:24-25)

"HEAVEN AND EARTH SHALL PASS AWAY
BUT MY WORDS SHALL NOT PASS AWAY"